IT CAN DAMAGE YOUR HEALTH

by Eric Chappell

SAMUEL FRENCH

FOR AMATEUR PRODUCTION ENQUIRIES

UNITED KINGDOM AND WORLD
EXCLUDING NORTH AMERICA
licensing@concordtheatricals.co.uk
020-7054-7298

Each title is subject to availability from Concord Theatricals,
depending upon country of performance.

The moral right of Eric Chappell to be identified as author of this work has been asserted in accordance with Section 77 of the Copyright, Designs and Patents Act 1988.

USE OF COPYRIGHTED MUSIC

A licence issued by Concord Theatricals to perform this play does not include permission to use the incidental music specified in this publication. In the United Kingdom: Where the place of performance is already licensed by the PERFORMING RIGHT SOCIETY (PRS) a return of the music used must be made to them. If the place of performance is not so licensed then application should be made to PRS for Music (www.prsformusic.com). A separate and additional licence from PHONOGRAPHIC PERFORMANCE LTD (www.ppluk.com) may be needed whenever commercial recordings are used. Outside the United Kingdom: Please contact the appropriate music licensing authority in your territory for the rights to any incidental music.

USE OF COPYRIGHTED THIRD-PARTY MATERIALS

Licensees are solely responsible for obtaining formal written permission from copyright owners to use copyrighted third-party materials (e.g., artworks, logos) in the performance of this play and are strongly cautioned to do so. If no such permission is obtained by the licensee, then the licensee must use only original materials that the licensee owns and controls. Licensees are solely responsible and liable for clearances of all third-party copyrighted materials, and shall indemnify the copyright owners of the play(s) and their licensing agent, Concord Theatricals Ltd., against any costs, expenses, losses and liabilities arising from the use of such copyrighted third-party materials by licensees.

IMPORTANT BILLING AND CREDIT REQUIREMENTS

If you have obtained performance rights to this title, please refer to your licensing agreement for important billing and credit requirements.

NOTE

Professional productions of **IT CAN DAMAGE YOUR HEALTH** have been licensed in the Middle and Far East, Australia and New Zealand using the title **ONLY WHEN I LAUGH**. Amateur productions in these territories may be presented using either title; *all* productions elsewhere *must* use the title **IT CAN DAMAGE YOUR HEALTH.**

Other plays by Eric Chappell published by
Samuel French Ltd

Haunted
Natural Causes
Theft

IT CAN DAMAGE YOUR HEALTH

First presented at the Churchill Theatre, Bromley, in association with Mark Furness, Alexander E. Racolin and Annette Moskowitz, on 11th October 1995, with the following cast:

Higgins	Michael Elphick
Palmer	Geoffrey Davies
Gary	Paul Venables
Gibbs	Tim Brierley
Ranji	Rohit Gokani
Christine	Jane Robbins

Directed by Robert Chetwyn
Designed by Peter Rice
Lighting by Leonard Tucker

CHARACTERS

Higgins, patient, mid-50s
Palmer, patient, about 40
Gary, patient, early 20s
Gibbs, Senior House Surgeon, about 40
Ranji, male nurse
Christine, nurse, 20s
Porter, non-speaking, any age
Patient, non-speaking, young

The action of the play takes place in a small hospital ward

Time — the present

SYNOPSIS OF SCENES

ACT I

ACT II

ACT I

A small hospital ward. Late morning

There are two doors: one, UL, leads to the nurses' station and the other, further DS, to the corridor. There are three beds in the ward: two are in line US, the third UR at right angles to the other two. Between the beds are cabinets and the usual medical equipment. There are lamps, flowers, jugs of water, glasses and get well cards on the cabinets, and, on the cabinet next to the bed L, a mirror; on that next to the bed C, a medical dictionary. Each bed has a clipboard of notes on it and can be curtained off. A table and chairs are arranged DL

When the Curtain *rises, Palmer is lying in the bed L, which has curtains drawn about it; Christine is with him. The adjacent bed is empty. Gary, a pale young man in his early twenties, is sitting apprehensively on the edge of the bed UR. He is wearing a dressing gown and clutching a bag of fruit and a bottle in a fancy wrapping. There is a teddy bear beside him*

Palmer groans behind the curtains. Gary starts nervously. A second groan follows

Higgins enters painfully. He groans, echoing the groan behind the curtain. He is in his mid fifties, burly and aggressive, and wears a dressing gown. He stops when he sees Gary and stares

Higgins Wrong room, mate.
Gary No – I don't think so. I was brought here.
Higgins Then where's Seymour?
Gary Seymour? I don't know.
Higgins I haven't seen him since last night.
Gary Perhaps he's gone home.
Higgins After open heart surgery? He wasn't going anywhere. Very delicate operation.
Gary Yes, I suppose it is.
Higgins Like having the back off a watch, things are never the same again.
Gary No. Still, you have to look on the bright side.
Higgins (*staring*) What bright side?
Gary At least he's in the right place.

Higgins (*amused*) Who told you that? (*He begins searching through the cabinet by Gary's bed*) He's gone all right. His Mintoes are missing. He wouldn't have gone without those. Sucked them all day. Not that he ever offered me one. I hate meanness — especially in hospital ….

Gary (*glancing down at his bag of fruit*) Would you like an orange?

Higgins Thanks. (*He takes an orange and begins to peel it. He studies it for a moment. Darkly*) I never thought I'd envy an orange.

Gary Why do you envy an orange?

Higgins (*splitting the orange*) They don't feel pain …

Gary Oh.

Higgins Fancy him going without saying goodbye.

Gary Perhaps he's gone to another ward.

Higgins Could have done. I've been down in X-ray for hours. If I have any more I'll be lighting up in the dark.

Palmer groans behind the curtains

They may have moved him because of Palmer. That groaning can be very wearing.

Gary Is it serious?

Higgins Take a look.

Gary I don't like to.

Higgins He won't mind – he likes an audience.

Gary peers behind the curtains and withdraws quickly

Gary He's having a massage.

Higgins I know – treats this place like a health farm. He shouldn't be in with the serious cases. He's a hypochondriac.

Gary If he's a hypochondriac why did they admit him?

Higgins Had to. He collapsed outside the hospital. Only way to get a bed these days. Go to the hospital of your choice and collapse outside. Mind you, it's the first time it's happened outside here – they usually collapse inside.

Christine, an attractive nurse in her twenties, emerges from behind the curtains. Giggling and flushed she adjusts her cap and exits

Higgins watches Gary's reaction with interest

Higgins Nice.

Gary Yes.

Higgins Your sort?

Gary (*awkwardly*) I don't know.

Higgins My God. If I was joined up properly …
Gary Yes.
Higgins Palmer's setting his stall out.
Gary Is he?
Higgins Thinks he's irresistible. Actually, you'd be more her type.
Gary (*startled*) Would I?
Higgins Oh, yes. Do you want me to put a word in?
Gary (*abruptly*) No. I mean — I'm not feeling very well.
Higgins What are you in for?
Gary I've had a lot of pain down here.
Higgins (*interested*) Lower abdomen?
Gary Yes.
Higgins You're in trouble.
Gary Am I?
Higgins Very complicated down there. You've got your gall bladder —
your pancreas — your spleen — your duodenum and your intestines. Do
you know how long your intestines are? Twenty-five feet. You could
stretch them across this room.
Gary (*returning to his bed and sitting; faintly*) They said it might be my
appendix.
Higgins They always say that.
Gary They say it doesn't serve any purpose: we don't use it.
Higgins Well, there are a few things we don't use but we don't want them
whipping out, do we? Are you having surgery?
Gary Yes. They said they wanted a peep.
Higgins A peep. You're going to have a laparotomy, that's what you're
going to have.
Gary Am I?

There is a pause

Higgins Do you want to see something horrible?
Gary What?
Higgins Do you want to see something — really horrible?
Gary I'm not sure …
Higgins Come here …

*Gary approaches Higgins. Higgins faces Gary and opens his dressing gown
slowly and dramatically*

Gary (*shocked*) Crikey!
Higgins They told me they were going to take a peep; turned out to be a
flaming coach trip — forty-five stitches. (*Darkly*) Exploratory.
Gary Exploratory?

Higgins That means they don't know what they're looking for and they wouldn't know what it was if they found it. And that's not the end of it. (*Broodingly*) I'm not right down here. You can always tell. I'm not joined up properly. I can't cough. I daren't. It's more than my life's worth. If I coughed I'd split. My skin doesn't fit me any more. I've been mutilated by the National Health Service. Who's doing you?
Gary Gibbs.

Higgins raises his eyebrows

He seemed all right.
Higgins You haven't met him with a knife in his hand.
Gary I think I'll lie down. I'm feeling a bit faint ... (*He gets into bed*)

Gibbs enters. He is the Senior House Surgeon. He is about forty. He looks weary and appears to be suffering from a hangover. He is followed by Christine

Gibbs The notes, nurse.

Christine hands Gibbs Gary's notes. He studies them and then sighs and puts a hand to his forehead

Yes, I see ... Now, Gary, let me have a look at you ... (*He reaches into the bed and finds himself holding the teddy bear. He stares down at Gary*)
Gary Er, they bought it at the office — it was for good luck.
Higgins (*quietly*) I'd hang on to it.

Gibbs glances sharply at Higgins, then returns to Gary and begins to examine him

Gibbs Hm .... Yes ... See the swelling, nurse.

Christine peers down. Gary looks embarrassed and turns away.

(*Pulling Gary back*) I don't think we can put this off. How do you feel, Gary?
Gary Much better.
Gibbs (*wearily*) Well, I'm glad one of us does.
Christine Can I get you something, Mr Gibbs?
Gibbs No, it'll pass.
Christine (*smiling*) It was quite a party.
Gibbs (*smiling back*) It certainly was.

Christine It must have been four o'clock.
Gibbs As late as that ...

During the following he continues to examine Gary whilst flirting with Christine

Christine I thought you were so funny when you put that traffic cone on your head and danced in the middle of the road.
Gibbs (*purring*) Did I do that?

Gary listens in horror

Christine I hope you weren't in trouble when you got home.
Gibbs (*frowning*) No, that was reserved for this morning. She doesn't understand. I'm a surgeon. I spend most of my time thrashing around in people's guts. I have to unwind. There is a life outside this hospital. The consultants are skiing in Austria. (*Muttering*) I just hope it bloody thaws.
Christine I can see you're in a mood.
Gibbs Yes. Well, I cut myself shaving this morning — then I scraped my car on the gate as I drove out. I knew it was going to be one of those days ... (*He turns his attention to Gary. Brightly*) Nothing to worry about, Gary. Everything's fine. We're going to take you down to the theatre and have a look around and if we see something we don't like we're going to snip it off. (*He moves to leave*)
Gary Oh, Mr Gibbs — Mother asked me to give you this. (*He hands Gibbs the bottle in the fancy wrapping*)
Gibbs (*smiling*) Oh. Do I know your mother?
Gary Yes. You did her gall bladder two years ago. She thinks you're wonderful.
Gibbs (*pleased*) Oh, thank you. I'm glad we have one satisfied customer. What is it? Nothing too strong I hope.
Gary No. It's my urine sample.
Gibbs (*frowning*) Are you trying to be funny?
Gary (*startled*) No.
Gibbs (*handing the bottle to Christine*) Keep your eye on him — I think he's half-witted.

He moves to leave again

Palmer appears from behind his curtains. He is a man about forty, pale and moustached, and with a languid air. At the moment he is supporting himself bravely by holding on to the curtains

Palmer Oh, Mr Gibbs.

Gibbs Yes, Palmer?

Palmer I wondered if there was any news of my pacemaker.

Gibbs Pacemaker? What pacemaker? (*He consults his notes*) There's nothing here about a pacemaker …

Ranji, an Indian male nurse, enters from the nurses' station

Staff.

Ranji Yes, Mr Gibbs?

Gibbs What's all this about a pacemaker?

Ranji He seems to think he needs a pacemaker.

Gibbs (*staring at Palmer*) Why should you think that?

Palmer I should have thought the reason was obvious – the reason I collapsed. I have a tired heart.

Gibbs (*briefly*) You have a tired body, Palmer – they go together. There's nothing wrong with your heart.

Palmer Then what is it? You can tell me. What is the real problem?

Gibbs We don't know the real problem – that's why we're running the tests. Up to now we've found nothing wrong with you.

Higgins (*softly*) Surprise. Surprise.

Palmer Nothing wrong with me? This is great news. (*He totters bravely towards Gibbs*) You mean I'll be able to lead an active life again?

Gibbs (*doubtfully*) Well, yes – that's if you led one before.

Palmer (*dramatically*) Then perhaps you can answer me one final question. Why can't I cross this room?

Gibbs I don't know.

Palmer I do: I need a pacemaker. Is it too much to ask? I know you have to watch your profit margins but it's not as if you don't get it back … afterwards. Don't want me exploding in the crematorium, do we? I'm only borrowing it. Or is it too late? Am I too far gone? Aren't I worth the trouble? (*He holds on to Gibbs' coat*)

Gibbs (*trying to pull away*) Er, yes … I think we'll have to change your medication, Palmer.

Ranji and Christine gently disengage Palmer and return him to his bed

Gibbs moves to the door, turns and gives Gary a withering glance

Right. Nurse. Staff. He's on my list for this morning. Get him ready and make sure he's well sedated — he seems unduly apprehensive.

Ranji, Christine and Gibbs turn and stare at Gary and then exit, leaving the patients alone

Gary I don't think he likes me.

Palmer You shouldn't have given him that bottle – there could have been a dreadful mistake. Imagine, that could have been washing down a lightly grilled Dover sole.

Gary They said bring a sample.

Higgins A sample! It looked like a year's supply. You only need a small bottle.

Gary I tried that. I had trouble with the neck …

Palmer I always use a tonic bottle.

Higgins You see – that gives him a social advantage straight away. They'll have him down for a gin and tonic man.

Palmer And what do you use: an old beer bottle?

Higgins I don't seek preferential treatment.

Palmer If I'm getting preferential treatment why can't I have a pacemaker?

Higgins Because you don't need one.

Palmer Of course I need one; I'm running down, you idiot. Can't you see that?

Higgins (*indignantly*) Who are you calling an idiot?

Gary (*anxiously*) No need to fall out; we're all in the same boat.

Higgins No, we're not. You're the one who's having the operation.

Gary He said there was nothing to worry about.

Higgins They all say that. Why do you think they wear those masks?

Gary I thought it was to prevent germs.

Higgins No – it's so you don't know who's done it. It's like a meeting of the Ku Klux Klan down there …

Ranji enters with a bowl and shaving utensils and puts them by Gary's bed

Ranji Have you been this morning?

Gary Been where?

Ranji Have you passed a motion?

Higgins Yes, a vote of no confidence.

Gary Oh, yes. Yes, I've been.

Ranji Good — at least you didn't bring that in a fancy wrapper …

Ranji exits

Gary He doesn't like me either.

Higgins He doesn't like anyone. He won't be happy until all the patients are replaced by dummies from Burton's window.

Gary (*staring at the bowl*) What's that for?

Higgins He's going to shave you.

Gary (*feeling his chin*) I've had one.

Higgins Not where he's going to shave you.

Gary Oh.

Higgins How do you feel?

Gary Nervous.

Higgins You've every right to be. You know what we are, don't you? We're the Kamikaze of the National Health Service. We should go down to that theatre with flags around our heads shouting "Banzai."

Gary It's not as bad as that, surely.

Higgins No, it's worse. All they had to do was dive on aircraft carriers – and they got geisha girls and saki. We have to do this on boiled fish and visits from the WRVS.

Palmer Don't listen to Higgins. Gibbs is an excellent surgeon.

Gary I know – everyone says so.

Higgins Of course they do. He's buried his mistakes.

Gary My mother says he has a gift for healing. She says he's made the sick walk.

Higgins Yeah, and he's made a few of them run before now but what does that prove?

Palmer Don't worry, Gary. Gibbs is thoroughly professional.

Higgins What do you know about it? You haven't been down there.

Palmer That's because it's too late. (*He sighs*) The sands of time are running out for Charlie Palmer.

Higgins Oh, my Gawd.

Gary They say there's nothing wrong with you.

Palmer Of course they do. They're trying to reassure me but I know. I'm burnt out. I've been too rash. I've abused my body – that's why I'm here, Gary.

Gary (*miserably*) Well, I haven't abused my body and I'm here. I'm beginning to wish I had. At least I'd have had something to think about.

Palmer Don't wish that. There's still time for you. If only I'd taken care – treated my body like a temple instead of the Savoy Grill. If only I'd had the check-ups and the screenings …

Higgins It's just your luck. I had an uncle once who went to East Africa. He took every precaution. He had injections for malaria, beriberi, blackwater fever, sleeping sickness, typhoid and cholera. He'd only been there a few days and an elephant trod on him.

Christine enters and hangs a chart on Gary's bed. She smiles at the men and exits

Palmer Well, I tell you one thing — I'm going to have that nurse before I go.

Gary (*uneasily*) You shouldn't be talking like that.

Palmer Why not?

Gary You're supposed to be ill.

Palmer I know but I don't seem to have lost that particular urge.

Higgins Then I suggest you do, Charlie, or you could get a sharp rap from the blunt end of a pair of scissors — where it hurts most. I've known it happen.

Gary groans

What's the matter?

Gary I feel terrible.

Palmer You'll be all right once you've had the operation.

Higgins Don't be too sure. You've seen what they did to me. I'm not joined up properly. I'm taking legal advice.

Palmer Well, you seem to have pulled through all right. You've never stopped talking.

Higgins That's my working-class ability to endure pain and suffering. Besides, I had mine on a Wednesday: this is Monday.

Gary What's Monday got to do with it?

Higgins It's just after the weekend, isn't it? Tuesday he's picking up. Wednesday he's fine. Thursday he's thinking about the weekend again. Friday he's off. Monday he's knackered. Mind you, with the appendix you do have an advantage.

Gary What's that?

Higgins There's only one of them. He usually gets confused when there's two to choose from.

Ranji enters looking grim; he carries a patient's consent form and a pen

Ranji (*to Gary*) You haven't signed the form.

Gary What form?

Ranji The consent form for the operation. You haven't signed it. Why didn't you say?

Gary I didn't know it was important.

Ranji Of course it's important. Suppose something went wrong? Where would we be then?

Gary Yes, of course, I'd better sign. (*He takes the paper, then hesitates*) What could go wrong?

Ranji Wrong? Nothing's going to go wrong. The chances of anything going wrong … (*He shrugs*)

Gary (*hopefully*) Astronomical?

Ranji A thousand to one.

Gary A thousand to one. As much as that. (*He is about to sign, then hesitates*) Suppose I'm the one?

Ranji You won't be.
Gary But suppose I am?
Ranji Then all will be well because you've signed the form.
Gary That won't do me much good. (*He signs the paper*)

Ranji takes the paper and exits

Still, I suppose a thousand to one's not bad.
Higgins That depends on who's the one, doesn't it? I don't think our erstwhile friend Seymour would agree.
Palmer Seymour?
Higgins (*darkly*) He's disappeared, hasn't he?
Palmer Yes. It must have been when I had my curtains drawn. I didn't hear anything.
Higgins You wouldn't. Probably came with the meat wagon – wheels greased for silent running and two body snatchers in plimsolls …

Christine enters with a sharp-looking razor

Gary watches Christine apprehensively. She smiles at him, places the razor on his locker and then moves to the door. All the men watch her

Palmer Christine. What's happened to Seymour?
Christine He's gone to another hospital.
Palmer Why?
Christine (*grinning*) He wasn't feeling very well …

She exits

Palmer Did you hear that? I like a girlfriend with a sense of humour.
Higgins (*drily*) She'd probably need one.
Gary Well, that's a relief. I thought she was going to shave me.
Palmer I don't think she could stand the excitement, Gary.
Higgins No, it'll be Ranji. He's trained for it. He used to be in the Gurkhas.
Gary What?

Ranji enters. He pulls back Gary's sheets and begins to apply the lather. Gary does his best to screen himself from view. Higgins and Palmer watch with evident enjoyment

Higgins Now do you see what I mean? It's started — the indignity, the humiliation. Talk about your life in their hands — you didn't know it was going to be your sex life, did you?
Gary You will be careful?

Ranji Of course I'll be careful. I haven't cut one of these off for a long time. (*He takes up the razor and begins to apply it to Gary's body*)

Higgins Well, just let's hope it isn't the end of a winning streak. It may not seem much to you but that's his pride and joy you've got there – and I don't like the way your hand is shaking.

Gary What!

Ranji (*flashing the razor in Higgins' direction*) My hand is not shaking. (*He lowers the razor on to Gary*)

Gary watches the movements of the razor with sick fascination

Higgins God – you've only been in the country five minutes and you're suffering from it already.

Ranji (*withdrawing the razor*) Suffering from what?

Higgins Emotional stress, mate.

Ranji I'm not suffering from emotional stress. (*He waves the razor angrily*) Now be quiet and get back to bed.

Higgins (*grumbling*) "Be quiet – get back into bed." That's all I ever hear. You know your trouble: you don't want to get to know us as people, do you?

Ranji Not particularly.

Higgins No: that's because we've joined the sub-species of the unwell. We're beneath your dignity.

Ranji I cannot afford to get involved with the patients.

Higgins Why not? It might do you some good. Just because you've taken our clothes it doesn't mean you've taken our identity. I bet you don't even know our names.

Ranji Of course I know your names.

Higgins No, you don't. He's the appendicitis in the corner, I'm the post-operative infection, and Charlie's the hypochondriac in the end bed.

Palmer Who's a hypochondriac? I'm not a hypochondriac. (*To Ranji*) Have you been calling me a hypochondriac?

Ranji No, I have not called you a hypochondriac. Will you both shut up and let me get on with my work. (*He makes another sweep with the razor*)

Higgins All right. All right. Stop waving that razor about; you could cut someone's ear off, or worse.

Gary What! (*He hurriedly gets out of bed and slips on his dressing-gown*)

Ranji Where are you going?

Gary Home.

Ranji But you're having an operation.

Gary No, I've changed my mind. I want antibiotics.

Christine enters with a tablet

Ranji Now look what you've done, Higgins.

Christine What's the matter?

Ranji (*hissing*) The appendicitis has refused his operation.

Christine You'd better tell Sister.

Ranji exits hurriedly

Gary, you can't do this.

Gary I want my clothes.

Christine But you must have the operation.

Higgins Wait a minute – it's his decision. He's got a perfect right to refuse the operation.

Christine (*moving to Higgins*) Not if it's going to cost him his life.

Higgins (*uneasily*) It won't come to that, will it? He doesn't look too bad to me.

Palmer I'm not so sure … (*He moves to Gary and studies him closely*) My Uncle George went that colour. He wouldn't listen.

Gary Wouldn't he have the operation?

Palmer It wouldn't have done him much good. He was dead when he went that colour. But he still looked better than you do, Gary.

Christine Sit down, Gary, and take this tablet. (*She pours Gary a glass of water*)

Gary I'm not being drugged.

Higgins You won't feel anything — I didn't. It's extracted from rocket fuel; sends you straight into orbit.

Gary (*hesitating*) You didn't feel anything? No pain?

Higgins No. (*He pauses*) That comes afterwards.

Palmer (*sharply*) Higgins.

Christine Gary, you must have the operation.

Gary Why? A lot of people refuse operations: Jehovah's Witnesses, Christian Scientists, faith healers …

Christine But you're C of E.

Gary But what about Gibbs? He cut himself shaving this morning; I could be next.

Christine Mr Gibbs is an experienced surgeon and this is a routine operation.

Palmer He has a fine reputation, Gary.

Gary Yes, and we know why, don't we? Because he's buried his mistakes.

Higgins Who told you that?

Gary You did. And you said you weren't joined up properly.

Christine (*sighing*) Higgins!

Higgins All right, they were a bit careless with the needlework; they should have put in a gusset. But I didn't refuse the operation, did I? That would have been suicidal.

Christine Mr Gibbs may have an abrupt manner but underneath he's gentle and caring; he's not a butcher.
Gary (*hesitating, then taking the glass from Christine*) Well, if you're sure ....

Gibbs strides in. He is wearing a theatre gown streaked with blood

Gibbs Now, Gary – what's all this?
Gary (*staring*) Oh, my God!

Gary drops the glass and exits hurriedly

Christine Gary!

Ranji and Christine follow Gary off

Gibbs What's the matter with the boy? He appears to be terrified. What's got into him?
Higgins (*innocently*) I've no idea. He's been like that ever since he arrived. Nervous, verging on the hysterically frightened. I can't understand it ...

Gibbs gives Higgins a searching look

Christine returns without the tablet

Gibbs Well?
Christine He's locked himself in the toilet. He's flushing the cistern and shouting for his clothes. Perhaps if you had a word with him, Mr Gibbs?
Gibbs If you think I'm going to shout my head off over a lavatory pan you're mistaken, nurse. Can we get in touch with his mother?
Christine I don't think so. She said she was going to church.
Gibbs Church?
Christine To pray for him.
Gibbs Well, that seems to show a general lack of confidence all round. It would appear I'm doing for surgery what Crippen did for medicine. And I'd like to know what gave Gary that impression and what's made him so apprehensive ...

Everyone stares at Higgins

Higgins (*shifting uneasily*) Well, I don't suppose it's that serious — if he doesn't have it.
Gibbs That depends on what you mean by serious. If he doesn't have the operation he'll probably die.

Palmer (*drily*) That sounds fairly serious.
Gibbs His position could become critical but not as critical as yours, Higgins. I hold you responsible for this. The boy is obviously susceptible to your mordant sense of humour.
Higgins (*staring*) Mordant?
Gibbs Well, you've talked him out of it: you can talk him back into it. I'll be waiting.

Gibbs stalks out followed by Christine

Higgins Mordant. What does mordant mean, Charlie?
Palmer Corrosive and biting.
Higgins (*impressed*) Get away.

Gary returns. He is carrying a small bag

Higgins You can't do it, Gary.
Gary I'm doing it.
Higgins What's the matter – you're not afraid, are you?
Gary (*astonished*) Of course I'm afraid. You said we should go down to the theatre with flags round our heads shouting "Banzai."
Higgins You don't want to take any notice of me; that's just my mordant sense of humour.
Palmer You heard what Ranji said, Gary – the odds against anything going wrong are a thousand to one.
Gary Yes, and with my luck I'll be the one.
Higgins (*considering this*) Suppose I could lengthen the odds?
Gary You can't.
Higgins Suppose I could: would it make a difference?
Gary (*hesitating*) I suppose so.
Higgins (*moving to Gary and going through his bag*) Right. Sit on the bed. (*He produces a yellow sock from the bag*) Now, put that yellow sock on.
Gary What?
Higgins Do as I tell you.
Gary All right. But I don't see the point. (*He puts on the sock*)
Higgins (*producing a red sock*) You will. Now put this red one on.
Gary Higgins, this is ridiculous.
Higgins It may be but I've lengthened the odds.
Gary (*staring at his feet*) How?
Higgins Ever heard of a patient wearing odd socks dying under the anaesthetic? I haven't. Have you, Charlie?
Palmer (*smiling*) No. The odds must be astronomical.
Higgins A million to one. In fact that phenomenon has never been encountered in the history of medicine.

Palmer He's right, Gary.

Higgins And just to make absolutely sure I'll throw in the teddy bear. (*He shoves the teddy bear under Gary's arm*) Now, ever heard of a case of a patient wearing odd socks and clutching a teddy bear dying under the knife, Charlie?

Palmer Never.

Higgins That's because it's never happened.

Gary hesitates and sits on the bed

Gary This doesn't make sense.

Higgins Of course it doesn't make sense; that's statistics for you. But you're not a statistic, you're an individual, Gary.

Christine enters carrying a surgical gown, with a porter wheeling a trolley. They stand by the door

Gary (*swallowing*) I know and I'm a very scared individual, Higgins.

Higgins I know you are. (*He lowers his voice*) We all are. But don't show it. She's watching you, sizing you up, seeing what you're made of ...

Christine Well, Gary?

Gary (*bravely*) Yes. I'm ready now, Christine. Could I have the tablet?

Ranji enters with the tablet

Gary takes the tablet. Christine holds up the surgical gown. Gary takes off his jacket and slips the gown on

Christine And the trousers, Gary.

Gary slips off his trousers. Higgins hands him the teddy bear. Gary climbs on to the trolley

Gibbs enters

Higgins He's ready for you now, doctor.

Gibbs Good. (*He moves to Gary*) Now, Gary, I don't want you to worry about a ... (*He stops and stares down at the socks*)

Higgins Do you mind if he goes down like this, Mr Gibbs?

Gibbs Well, they're a little garish for my taste but I don't see why not. Anything to get him down there. And the teddy bear as well, I suppose?

Higgins If you don't mind. Just for luck.

Gibbs Sometimes I find your confidence in me quite moving, Higgins. Very well. I'll see you down there, Gary. You and our furry friend ...

Gibbs exits

The porter starts to move the trolley off

Gary (*anxiously*) I will be all right, won't I?
Christine You'll be fine, Gary.
Higgins Of course you will.
Palmer Good luck, Gary.

The trolley moves towards the door

Higgins Yeh, see you, Gary. (*He pauses*) All being well …

Gary raises himself up and stares

CURTAIN

SCENE 2

The ward. Three days later. Late evening

When the CURTAIN *rises, Palmer is at the table, idly shuffling cards*

Higgins enters wearily and joins him

Higgins Don't you think I'm a funny colour?
Palmer (*studying Higgins*) I don't know. I don't know what colour you
    were before.
Higgins Better than this, mate. I'm a funny colour and it's getting worse.
Palmer (*mournfully*) You're lucky to have a colour. I'm just sort of beige.
    They think it may be chronic fatigue syndrome. It would account for my
    lethargy.
Higgins Chronic fatigue syndrome? (*He shakes his head*) Whatever hap-
    pened to tiredness? (*He looks around*) Where's Gary?
Palmer (*archly*) Christine's taken him for a bath.
Higgins That should be fun.
Palmer He's making very slow progress, isn't he?
Higgins He likes the attention. Have you noticed the way he leans on her
    arm. I think he fancies her.
Palmer I thought he had a girlfriend.
Higgins No.
Palmer Then who does he write to all the time? He never stops.

Higgins He's not writing to anyone. He never tears the pages out. He's never had a girlfriend. He told me.

Palmer Well, that explains it.

Higgins What do you mean?

Palmer I have a theory about him.

Higgins What?

Palmer Yellow socks.

Higgins Yeah?

Palmer Teddy bear.

Higgins Yeah?

Palmer Holidays with his mother …

Higgins So?

Palmer I think he's gay.

Higgins What! Just because the poor bugger wears yellow socks and has a teddy bear.

Palmer You must admit it's effeminate.

Higgins No, I don't. What about the Battle of Britain? Half those young pilots got into their Spitfires with teddy bears under their arms — no one called them effeminate. And he holidays with his mother because his father's snuffed it. You want to watch what you're saying.

Palmer (*staring at Higgins curiously*) You seem very concerned about him.

Higgins Well, someone has to be. He doesn't know the ropes, does he? And he sort of looks up to me.

Palmer You?

Higgins (*defiantly*) Yeh.

Palmer He must be desperate. Haven't you got enough kids of your own?

Higgins All girls. Filled the house with them trying to get a boy.

Palmer My God. I think you're going to adopt him.

Higgins All I said was —— (*He breaks off*)

Gary enters

Where's Christine?

Gary Called away. I had to walk back on my own. I feel terrible. (*He slumps on to the bed*)

Higgins That's because you're ill.

Gary I think I'm going to die.

Higgins Of course you're not.

Palmer You worry too much, Gary. It comes to all of us – it's perfectly natural.

Higgins There's nothing natural about dying – you try holding your breath.

Palmer It wouldn't worry me. You see, I believe. You don't believe, do you, Ray?

Higgins I believe that when you're dead you're dead. Religion is the opiate of the people. They all say it's going to be wonderful up there but I don't see any of them rushing to go.

Palmer You wouldn't talk like that if you'd had my experience. I've seen Him.

Higgins Who?

Palmer God. When I had my first attack.

Gary (*impressed*) What did he look like?

Palmer Actually, he looked rather like my bank manager.

Higgins Of course he did — you collapsed in Barclays.

Palmer (*dreamily*) He had a friendly smile and twinkling eyes. And he spoke to me through a sort of mist.

Gary What did he say?

Palmer He said, "Not now, Charlie. Not now. Go back. Go back." It was a wonderful experience.

Higgins Yes, well, you wait until he says, "Come here. Come here." You might feel differently then.

Christine enters. She puts a small tape recorder on the table

Christine I'll just leave it there for the moment …

Palmer (*nervously*) Is it for my heart?

Christine No, it's a tape recorder. I'm going to record your requests for the hospital radio later – when it's quiet.

Higgins That's a waste of time. I requested *I Recall a Gypsy Woman*, last week. They still haven't played it.

Christine (*grinning*) That's nothing. A man in geriatrics requested *Keep Right on to the End of the Road*. By the time we played it he'd been dead three days.

She exits

Palmer Did you see the way she looked at me. Did you see those eyes? I certainly wouldn't kick her out of bed for eating cream crackers …

Gary Why should you do that?

Palmer What?

Gary I don't understand. Why should you kick her out of bed for eating cream crackers? Does she eat cream crackers?

Palmer and Higgins exchange glances

Palmer Do you want to play cards, Ray?

Higgins Not after the last time. You know what happened.

Palmer Oh, yes.

Gary What happened?

Higgins The last time I played — and Charlie can verify this — I drew the nine of clubs in my first hand.

Gary Nine of clubs?

Higgins The death card.

Palmer You're so superstitious.

Higgins It doesn't pay to disregard these things. (*He picks up a magazine*) Let's see what my stars say … Sagittarius. (*Reading*) "You will receive several shock waves this month." That's putting it mildly. "Strangers will play a large part in your life." Well, they don't come any stranger than you two.

Palmer That could mean anything.

Higgins All right. What about this? (*Reading*) "You will meet someone who wants to see more of you." That's Gibbs. He's certainly seen more of me — inside and out.

Gary What does mine say?

Higgins What are you? No, don't tell me. You're a Virgo.

Gary No, I'm Aries the Ram.

Higgins You could have fooled me. I mean you're hardly typical. They're choleric and violent.

Palmer Well, he's hardly that.

Higgins Perhaps he's got hidden depths. Perhaps he's going to turn choleric and violent at any moment. After all, he shares that sign with Vincent Van Gogh, the well known ear slasher.

Gary What does it say?

Higgins (*reading*) "You will attend a glittering opening at the beginning of the month". There you are then.

Gary What do you mean there you are then?

Higgins That's when you had your operation.

Palmer What a load of balls. (*He pauses*) What does mine say?

Higgins What are you?

Palmer Scorpio.

Higgins That's a dark sign to be born under. Scorpios are prone to mental disorders and looseness of the bowels. You share it with Goebbels and Herman Goering.

Palmer That doesn't worry me because I don't believe in it.

Higgins That's a pity because it's quite good.

Palmer (*intrigued*) Is it?

Higgins Yes. (*Reading*) "You will make a stunning impact at this time if you have the courage to be different. You will experience some of your most ecstatic moments both sexually and emotionally but you must fight your inhibitions. Take good care of your skin and beware of drastic beauty treatments."

Palmer (*puzzled*) What? (*He moves to Higgins and takes the magazine*) This is a woman's magazine, Higgins!

Higgins Well, it was all I could find.

Ranji enters. He places a tray by Palmer's bed; on the tray is the equipment for taking a blood test

What's your star sign, Ranji? No — let me guess. You're Aquarius the water carrier.

Ranji (*indignantly*) I'm not a water carrier.

Higgins All right. When were you born?

Ranji First of October.

Higgins (*with mock sadness*) Ah, we've missed your birthday.

Ranji What?

Higgins October. You're a Libran.

Ranji I have no time for this nonsense.

Higgins Salt of the earth, Librans.

Ranji I am not ... (*He pauses*) Salt of the earth?

Higgins Well balanced and intelligent. Mahatma Gandhi was a Libran.

Ranji (*impressed*) Mahatma Gandi. I didn't know that.

Higgins Yes, and Bridget Bardot. Attractive and charming, Librans. It's a well known fact.

Ranji Really. Well, I suppose one should approach these things with an open mind.

Higgins And caring.

Ranji Well, that's me of course. (*He turns briskly to Palmer*) Roll up your sleeve I haven't got all day.

Palmer (*concerned*) What are you going to do with that syringe?

Ranji I want some of your blood.

Palmer (*alarmed*) Some of my blood. Have you done this before?

Ranji Of course I've done it before.

Palmer Well, be careful, I have very delicate veins. How much are you going to take?

Ranji I'm going to fill this syringe.

Palmer That's almost a cupful. I can't spare that. What do you want it for?

Ranji We want to check your calcium level.

Palmer Calcium level. Is there a deficiency? My God! That explains it. The little white marks behind the nails. The feeling of brittleness.

Ranji Clench your fist and stop making a fuss.

Palmer clenches his fist and Ranji begins the procedure

Palmer Be careful. I bruise very easily.

Ranji There — you didn't feel a thing.

Palmer Oh …

Ranji Now I'm drawing off the blood.

Palmer Ohhhh.

Ranji I always feel if a patient knows what's happening it reduces the tension.

Higgins Wanna bet?

Palmer My God! Haven't you got enough? You're draining me. I'm going. I can feel it. I'm going. I know I am … I'm going … (*He falls back on the pillow*)

Higgins He's gone.

Ranji What's the matter with you, Palmer?

Higgins He always does that at the sight of blood – especially his own.

Ranji (*sighing*) Wake up, Palmer. (*He taps Palmer lightly on the cheek*) My goodness. What an old woman.

Palmer (*opening his eyes*) Oh, I'm sorry. A moment's weakness, I'm afraid. I hope I didn't alarm you all.

Ranji Don't worry — you didn't. (*He moves to the door with the tray and smiles at Higgins*) Gentle and caring? There could be some truth in it …

He exits

Palmer Did you hear that? Calcium deficiency. It's more serious than they thought.

Higgins That's not serious.

Palmer Of course it is. I grind my teeth at night. I could be down to the gums by morning.

Higgins Look, the one good thing about being in hospital is that you can always find someone worse off than yourself.

Palmer Who?

Higgins Well, me for a start.

Palmer You're not worse off than me.

Higgins There's nothing wrong with you.

Palmer Of course there is.

Higgins Then why haven't you had any treatment?

Palmer Because there's nothing they can do. When I collapsed and they brought me in here they tied my tag around the ankle; they normally put it on the wrist. (*Darkly*) And you know what that means ….

Gary (*after a pause*) No — what does it mean?

Palmer It's for easy identification, Gary — for when they pull the drawer out.

Gary (*staring*) What would you be doing in a drawer?

Palmer I'd be dead, Gary.

Higgins You're not going to die. You'll see us all out. No, when I look around I can't see anyone worse off than me.

Gary What about the man in the end ward?

Higgins What about him?

Gary I heard the nurses talking when I was in the shower. There's nothing they can do – too advanced. They're sending him home.

Higgins Poor bugger. Is that the one with red hair and freckles or the one with two sticks?

Gary I don't know. They said he wasn't very old. They said it was tragic.

Higgins That's life I suppose.

Palmer No, actually, that's death, Higgins. You have to accept it.

Higgins Right. (*He considers*) End ward?

Gary Yes. After Cavendish.

Higgins (*pointing towards the door*) That's Cavendish ward.

Gary Yes — at the end.

Higgins (*after a pause; frowning*) There isn't a ward at the end, is there, Charlie?

Palmer No — that's Radiology.

Gary Then where's the end ward?

Higgins At the end of Cavendish?

Gary Yes.

Higgins Well, it must be this end.

Palmer You mean this is the end ward ….?

They stare at each other as the truth slowly dawns

Gary It's one of us.

Higgins Yes — it's me.

Palmer No — it's me.

Gary It could be me. They said he was young.

Higgins No. You're too young.

Gary (*bitterly*) I know I'm too young. You don't have to tell me that. I haven't done anything with my life. I've never had a girlfriend. I haven't even been abroad. I don't even go out much.

Higgins (*alarmed*) They can't send me home. Not to a mother-in-law, four kids and a wife who can't stand illness.

Palmer (*hopefully*) I suppose it could be a rumour?

Gary It was just something I overheard – just a snatch of conversation – I could have got it wrong.

Palmer Of course you got it wrong.

Ranji enters singing softly to himself and carrying a card

Ranji sounds cheerful enough.

Higgins Of course he does. He worships Kali. Goddess of death and destruction.

Ranji (*smiles*) I'll ignore that remark, Higgins, because I want you to sign this card before you leave.

Higgins (*suspiciously*) Who said I was leaving?

Ranji Well, you're not going to stay with us forever, are you? (*He hands the card to Higgins*)

Higgins What is it?

Ranji A kidney donor card. There's a desperate need — so if you could sign it ——

Higgins Desperate! Don't you think I'm desperate? Haven't you got any tact. Blimey! You can't wait, can you? Here I am fighting for my life and all you can see is a set of spare parts.

Ranji Well, if you feel like that … (*He turns to Gary*) What about you, Gary? Wouldn't you like to bequeath your kidneys to someone less fortunate than yourself?

Gary After I'm dead?

Ranji Yes.

Gary How can you be less fortunate than dead? I'm not signing it.

Palmer Why not, Gary? They won't be any good to you after you're dead. You could leave your kidneys, your heart and your lungs. After all, you said you wanted to get out more. You could travel to foreign parts – even have a girlfriend. It's a wonderful opportunity.

Gary Then why don't you sign?

Palmer I will. Leave it with me, Ranji.

Ranji (*putting the card on Palmer's locker*) Well, don't forget to sign it before you go …

Palmer Go? Go where?

Ranji Good news. You're going home at the weekend.

Ranji exits

Palmer What did he say?

Gary He said you were going home at the weekend …

Gary and Higgins regard Palmer thoughtfully

Palmer My God! It's me.

Higgins Never mind, Charlie — at least you've met Him.

Palmer Who?

Higgins The kindly figure with the twinkling eyes.

Palmer (*bitterly*) Yes. I was forgetting Him. (*He looks upwards*) Thank you, God. Nice one. So you've decided to give Charlie Palmer one last kick in the teeth. Why me? Why couldn't it have been Stringer?

Gary Who's Stringer?

Palmer My managing director — the little creep. He's got everything: personalized number plates, indoor pool, jacuzzi, Persian rugs, ivory chess set. And what have I got to show for my life? Nothing. He wouldn't even give me a seat on the board.

Higgins Well, let's face it, Charlie. No one's going to give you a seat on the board. You're a hypochondriac.

Palmer Don't be ridiculous, Ray. Who's ever heard of a dead hypochondriac?

Higgins You're not going to die.

Palmer You heard Ranji. I'm going home.

Higgins We're all going home.

Gary It could be any one of us.

Higgins The big thing is not to get depressed.

Gary Keep our spirits up.

Higgins Half the battle … (*He begins a mournful chorus of "I'm H.A.P.P.Y."*)

The others join in dolefully, first Gary, then Palmer. Their voices die away

Silence

Gary I think I'll be cremated.

Higgins What, now?

Gary No, when I'm dead.

Higgins Well, I won't. I don't fancy being stuck on the mantelpiece and used as an ashtray.

Gary No, I shall have them spread somewhere nice. A leafy stream, or a river, or even the sea.

Palmer Listen to him. He's still trying to get abroad.

Higgins Well, you have to be careful. We spread my uncle's ashes from the cross channel ferry. It was all right until the wind changed then half of him ended up in the sandwiches.

Gary Will you be cremated, Charlie?

Palmer No. We have a family vault in Sussex.

Higgins Did you hear that? You see, there's no equality, not even in death. There'll be no dog cocking a leg over his grave. Edie wants us to be buried together with the inscription "Together again — in death as in life." I suppose that means she'll be on top and we'll have to make room for her mother. I fancied something more personal myself …

Gary What's that?

Higgins No, you'll only laugh.

Gary No, go on.

Higgins A simple inscription. "Tread softly: here lies Ray Higgins. We shall not see his like again."

Palmer Well, that should reassure everyone.

Gary I think that's lovely.

Higgins It needs to be simple.

Gary What about: "Here lies Gary Duffin. God has picked a flower."

Palmer (*drily*) Oh, yes …

Higgins I think that's very tasteful. What about you, Charlie?

Palmer (*after a moment's hesitation*) Well, yes — I had thought of something. It was something I read. I hope it's not too sentimental …

Higgins Go on.

Palmer "Here lies Charlie Palmer. His life was gentle and the elements so mixed in him that nature might stand up and say to all the world, 'This was a man.'" (*He turns away emotionally*)

Gary That's beautiful.

Higgins God, this is depressing.

Palmer We can't go on like this. We have to know.

Gary I don't think I want to know.

Palmer Anything's better than this uncertainty.

Higgins Are you sure about that, Charlie?

Palmer Surely they'd tell us.

Higgins That depends on whether they think you can take it. They judge each case on its merits. If they don't think you can handle it they won't tell you. And after observing the blind panic around here I don't think they'll tell us.

Gary What will they do?

Higgins They'll tell a close relative.

Palmer I haven't got any close relatives. My wife left me years ago. I only have a few distant cousins.

Higgins It's going to be a quiet funeral then, Charlie.

Palmer They'd have to tell me, wouldn't they, Ray?

Higgins I suppose so. Although there are ways of knowing …

Gary How?

Higgins Certain things change.

Palmer What sort of things?

Higgins Well, people are much nicer to you once it gets around: everyone starts calling you by your first name, you have more visitors, relatives you haven't seen for years – like your distant cousins, Charlie. There'll be sudden, inexplicable outbursts of weeping. And if you were going to take a holiday next year they'll suggest you take it now. They'll keep telling you to live for the moment, that you never know what's around the corner. And no one will interrupt you while you're talking, and all your whims will be indulged.

Gary Just like the Kamikaze, Ray.

Higgins We are the Kamikaze, Gary.

Palmer You make it sound quite attractive.

Higgins Yes; the trouble is it doesn't last long.

Christine enters, moves to Gary, puts a hand on his brow and checks his pulse

Christine How are you feeling, Gary?
Gary (*suspiciously*) All right. Well, I'm not all right but I'm feeling better.
Christine Good. They said I should be especially nice to you.
Gary (*sharply*) Why?
Christine What?
Gary Why are you being especially nice to me?
Christine Because you've had an operation.
Gary (*pointing to Higgins*) So has he. Why aren't you being nice to him?
Christine (*puzzled*) I will be.
Higgins (*alarmed*) No need to be nice to me. I'm all right.
Christine (*smiling*) That's the first time I've heard you say that.
Palmer Well, you can be nice to me any time, Christine.
Christine I don't know about that — not after what Sister told me.
Palmer What did she say?
Christine She said you tried to kiss her.
Palmer (*archly*) Tried to kiss her. She forced herself on me while I was lying helpless under the influence of drugs.
Christine You haven't had any drugs.
Higgins He means the ones he brought in with him.
Christine (*smiling*) Well, you just behave yourself, Charlie …

She exits

Palmer I'm definitely getting somewhere there.
Higgins Yeh but is it your magnetic personality or is it because you're going to snuff it?
Palmer What!
Higgins She knows who it is. Bound to. She can't tell us of course — it's against the Hippocratic Oath. But she knows. All we have to do is watch her because you know what she is, don't you?
Palmer What?
Higgins She's your angel of death.
Gary Crikey!

Christine returns to remove the flowers

The men watch her every movement anxiously. Christine pauses by Palmer's bed and leans forward to straighten his pillow. He flinches

Christine Don't forget your request, Charlie.
Palmer Request?
Christine As long as it's not too complicated I'll try and satisfy it …

She exits

Palmer (*astonished*) Did you hear that?
Higgins She means for the hospital radio.
Gary She's doing special requests.
Higgins Yeh, it could be your last request.
Palmer (*concerned*) And she called me Charlie. She's never done that before.
Gary A last request. I hadn't thought of that. This could be my last chance to say something — my last recorded message. Something I could leave behind.
Palmer No it wouldn't because as soon as they'd played it they'd wipe the tape; you'd be recorded over.
Higgins Yeh, what an epitaph, Gary. "Here lies Gary Duffin; he was recorded over."
Gary They may not — not if it was particularly moving.
Higgins If you're going to be moving I'm off.

Christine enters and sits by Gary's bed with the tape recorder. She switches it on

Christine (*into the hand microphone*) I'm now speaking to Gary Duffin of Men's Surgical — in the end ward. Hallo, Gary.
Gary Hallo, Christine. (*With a wry smile*) *End* ward … rather ironic really.
Christine Er, yes. What would you like us to play for you, Gary?
Gary *Don't It Make My Brown Eyes Blue.*
Christine That's a very sad song, Gary.
Gary Just a wry comment on the bitter-sweet quality of life, Christine. I'm just sitting here thinking of what might have been … and if only … (*He sighs*) If only; the saddest words in the English language.
Higgins (*softly*) Oh Gawd.
Christine Yes … And would you like to dedicate it to someone?
Gary Yes.
Christine I thought so. And who's the lucky girl?
Gary My mother.
Christine Oh. That's nice. (*She moves away*)
Gary And my grandmother.

Christine returns to Gary

My Uncle George and Aunty Emily. Everyone at the office – we had some
great times. Think of me sometimes. And my family in Australia. I always
meant to come and see you, John. (*Emotionally*) Kiss the twins for me. (*He
hesitates*). I think that's it.

Higgins Sure there's no one in Kuala Lumpur you'd like to mention?

Gary Oh, I'd just like to add one more thing. Something that in the cut and
thrust of life we often forget. If you love someone — tell them. Don't leave
it too late …

Christine (*staring at him incredulously*) Er, yes. Thank you, Gary. That was
very moving. (*She moves to Palmer*) Do you have a request, Charlie
Palmer?

Palmer Yes, Christine. I've been reading a wonderful book. *War and
Peace*. Which tells us so much about the human condition and puts
everything into perspective. So I'd like the *1812 Overture* played by the
Moscow Symphony Orchestra with cannons and bells. I find it so full of
hope.

Christine And a dedication?

Palmer To you, Christine.

Christine Oh. Surely there's someone closer.

Palmer No; there was someone once but things didn't work out. Oh, I'm not
complaining. (*With a brave smile*) After all, what's life but a game played
by fools?

Higgins Gawd! Now he's off.

Palmer I've warmed my hands before the fire of life, it sinks and now I'm
ready to depart.

Higgins I wish you would.

Christine (*uncertainly*) The *1812 Overture* …

Palmer With cannons and bells.

Christine moves to the door

Higgins Hey! What about me?

Christine I thought we'd had yours. (*She returns to Higgins*)

Higgins I know but you haven't played it.

Christine What was it again?

Higgins *I Recall a Gypsy Woman.*

Christine (*grinning*) Well, I wish we could but we don't seem to be able to
find her.

Higgins That's typical of the incompetence of this hospital. (*He seizes the
microphone*) Not that I'm surprised — not after my operation. That was
bungled …

Gibbs enters from the corridor and exits into the nurses' station

If there's nothing wrong why am I having all these X-rays? I think they're looking for a scalpel. Gibbs always was a clumsy bugger …

Gibbs appears from the nurses' station, staring incredulously

During the following Christine turns to look at Gibbs

Well, I shall find out. I'll penetrate this wall of silence if it's the last thing I do. There's been a cover-up and I intend to get to the bottom of it … (*His voice tails away as he follows Christine's eye to where Gibbs is standing*)

Gibbs (*coldly*) What are you doing, nurse?

Christine I was recording some messages for the hospital radio.

Gibbs I suggest you do that in your own time. Now where are Palmer's notes from Haematology?

Christine I thought you had them, Mr Gibbs.

Gibbs If I had them I wouldn't be asking for them, would I? If you spent less time on your outside interests perhaps you'd know where they were.

Christine I'm sorry … I ——

Gibbs There's too much levity in this ward. These men should be resting, instead of which they seem to be padding about half the night. This is a hospital, nurse, not the Holiday Inn. Now find those notes.

Christine exits tearfully

Gary (*reproachfully*) She was crying.

Gibbs What?

Gary She was crying. There were tears in her eyes.

Gibbs There'll be tears in my eyes, Gary, if this continues.

Palmer (*quietly*) Oh, Mr Gibbs.

Gibbs Yes?

Palmer Are these what you're looking for? (*He holds up a file*)

Gibbs What are they?

Palmer My notes from Haematology. They were by my bed.

Gibbs How did they get there?

Palmer You left them there earlier this evening ….

The patients all regard Gibbs reproachfully

Gibbs (*uncomfortably*) Oh.

Christine returns

Everyone turns to look at Christine

Christine I'm sorry, Mr Gibbs. They're not on the desk. I don't know where they are ... I seem to have lost them ...

The patients all turn their gaze back from Christine to Gibbs

Gibbs No, you haven't. I mislaid them. I'm sorry. In my eagerness to apportion blame I chose the youngest and most junior member of the staff — one least able to defend herself. It was unforgivable. Let me make amends. Let me make you a cup of tea ...

Gibbs puts an arm on Christine's shoulder and they exit

Higgins Did you see that? He fancies her.
Gary No, he's a doctor.
Palmer They're trained to resist that sort of thing.
Higgins And what happens one day when they're examining a beautiful woman and the old stethoscope starts to twitch? Then it's "I'm sorry, my dear but I can't treat you professionally — you'll have to go somewhere else. The temptation's too strong." And she says "Don't worry about that — where do I put my clothes?" And he says, "On top of mine."
Gary Doctors aren't like that.
Higgins Don't you believe it. Some of them train seven years to become doctors. And when they qualify they work an eighty hour week for next to nothing. Why do you think they do that?
Gary Why?
Higgins For the crumpet.
Palmer Christine's not crumpet.
Gary No.
Higgins She's a nurse, isn't she? They're only in it for one thing.
Gary What's that?
Higgins The doctors. No, we shan't see them again this evening. Who's for a smoke?
Palmer We're not supposed to smoke in here.
Higgins What were you at school – a prefect? Come on – we've been abandoned for the night.

Higgins produces cigarettes; he and Palmer light up and inhale greedily. Palmer stands cautiously by the door

What about you, Gary?
Gary Why not? (*He takes a cigarette*) I always thought it would be bad for my health. (*He lights up clumsily*) I've never done this before.

Higgins (*studying Gary*) I can see that. You don't burn evenly. You won't
do any good until you burn evenly. And you're not taking it down. You
can't enjoy a cigarette if you don't take it down ... (*He inhales contentedly*)
Palmer Someone's coming!

*Palmer leaps into bed and hides his cigarette under the sheets. Higgins drops
his into the water jug*

  Gibbs enters. He sees Gary sitting in a cloud of smoke

Gibbs Gary! What do you think you're doing? You're not supposed to
smoke in here. (*He snatches the cigarette from Gary and stubs it out*) It's
a disgusting habit which can lead to lung cancer, respiratory problems,
thrombosis and an early death.
Gary (*aggrieved*) I only had a puff.
Gibbs That's one puff too many. Gary, I have had four friends die in early
middle age – three of them were heavy smokers.
Gary (*curiously*) What was the other one?
Gibbs (*considering*) He was a jogger.
Higgins I've always said jogging was bad for you. I've given it up.

Gibbs stares at Higgins suspiciously

Palmer suddenly leaps out of bed beating out his smoking bedclothes

Palmer Hell!

Gibbs sighs and makes for the door

Gary (*sulkily*) I notice you don't say anything to Palmer.
Gibbs I'm concerned with you, Gary. It's too late for Palmer.

  He exits

Palmer (*alarmed*) Did you hear that? Too late for Palmer. It is me.

Higgins moves to the door

Palmer Where are you going?
Higgins I'm going to find out.
Palmer How?
Higgins That night orderly's come on in Cavendish. I'll ask him. He knows
everything that goes on around here. Anything's better than this suspense.

Palmer Are you sure?
Higgins Yes. I want to know whether to book for my holidays, don't I?

He exits

Palmer and Gary watch Higgins' progress through the glass panel in the door

Palmer That's my epitaph, Gary. "Too late for Palmer … "
Gary It could be any of us, Charlie. Why should it be you?
Palmer Because I had this terrible dream last night. We were all in rowing boats on a boating lake. The three of us. My boat was number twenty-three – it was on the side. I can see it now. And this figure came to the edge of the water shrouded in mist and called out "Come in Number Twenty-three — your time is up."
Gary Was he the kindly figure with the twinkling eyes?
Palmer How do I know? The bugger was shrouded in mist. (*He peers closer through the glass*) Look. Higgins is talking to him. What are they saying? They're looking over here. My God, he's avoiding my eye. I feel like the condemned man.
Gary They say you can always tell if the verdict's guilty. The jury never look at the accused.
Palmer You're a great comfort I must say. He's coming back!

Higgins enters looking serious

Palmer (*with studied calm*) Well, Ray – what's the verdict? What did you find out?
Higgins (*avoiding Palmer's gaze*) Nothing – nothing at all. (*He moves to his bed, still refusing to look at Palmer*)
Palmer (*groaning*) I knew it. It's me, isn't it. Too late for Palmer … (*He slumps back on the bed*)
Higgins Sorry, Charlie, but it is only a rumour.
Palmer It's not a rumour, Ray. I've always known deep down.
Gary I'm sorry, Charlie.
Higgins If there's anything we can do.
Palmer It's too late, Ray. Too late for everything. I had such plans. Well, I won't get that seat on the board now. I just hope they're sorry. Stringer didn't even come to see me. Not even a get well card, not even one solitary grape. I've a good mind to tell him what to do with his job.
Gary Why don't you, Charlie? You've nothing to lose now — you're fireproof. They can't hurt you any more. Why don't you tell him to stick his job?

Higgins (*anxiously*) You can't — it's only a rumour.

Palmer Can't I? (*He takes a mobile phone from his bedside cabinet*)

Gary I didn't know you had one of those.

Palmer Of course you didn't, because the bugger's never rung. (*He savagely punches a number in*) Not one solitary phone call.

Higgins You can't use those in here, Charlie; they interfere with the equipment.

Palmer What were you at school, Higgins – a prefect?

Gary (*excitedly*) I'll keep watch, Charlie.

He exits into the corridor

Higgins limps after Gary and looks through the glass

Palmer (*into the phone*) Hallo, Stringer. It's me, Charlie Palmer, the man the world forgot. ... Listen: I'll call you Mr Stringer when you earn the title, you little creep. ... Yes, that's what I called you: a pint-sized, eighteen-carat creep. ... No, I'm not drunk. And you can't sack me because I quit. You can take your job and stick it. (*He laughs wildly across at Higgins*)

Higgins (*returning to Palmer and pulling at Palmer's sleeve; hissing*) Charlie — it's not you.

Palmer (*lowering the phone*) What?

Higgins (*nodding towards the door*) It's him.

Palmer Gary?

Higgins Yes. I had to say it was you or he'd have guessed. He was looking at me — I couldn't give the game away, could I?

Palmer Poor Gary.

Higgins Yes.

Palmer Then why do I feel so pleased?

Higgins That's human nature. You don't want these things to happen but if they do, let them happen to someone else.

Palmer When do you think they'll tell him?

Higgins Probably won't. Probably tell his mother. That should send her back to church with a few questions.

Palmer What questions?

Higgins Like, why him and not you.

Palmer They say the good die young, Ray.

Higgins That's because they haven't had time to be anything else. It doesn't seem fair, does it?

Palmer I know it's not fair but all I can feel at the moment is relief. I'm going to live. I'm going to ... (*He becomes aware of the mobile phone in his hand. He stares at Higgins and then back at the phone. Into the phone*) Mr Stringer? Did you hear that? I'm going to be all right. Mr Stringer, I've been very ill. I'm on very strong medication. It does have these side effects. So if I did say something … Mr Stringer? Mr Stringer …? (*He puts down the phone*)

Higgins Well, I think I'll have an early night. It's been a busy day … (*He slips into bed and switches off his light*)

Palmer groans

CURTAIN

ACT II

The ward. Two days later. Late evening

The flowers have returned and there is a sleeping tablet on each cabinet

Gary is in bed writing in his diary. Higgins and Palmer are at the table reading books. Higgins looks up from his paperback

Higgins This is nice.
Palmer What is?
Higgins Being able to read in peace and quiet. Nice, isn't it?
Palmer (*absently*) Yes.
Higgins You can almost hear it, can't you?
Palmer What?
Higgins The silence.
Palmer Yes.
Higgins That's the trouble today. Too much noise, even in hospital. It was like a fairground out there today. You can't even be ill in peace. In the old days they put straw down in the streets to silence the wheels when someone was ill — showed some respect. Different now; if you wanted to die in peace you'd need earmuffs.
Palmer I'm trying to read, Higgins.
Higgins You've picked the best time. You can't read in the day. Too many visitors, too many kids running about. One ran straight into my stitches this morning. Visitors. I remember when it was two hours a day and that was too much. They don't want to come and we don't want to see them. If the patients had a vote they'd keep the buggers out. (*He pauses*) No, it'll be quiet now, until the drunks and the drug addicts arrive, and the grievous bodily harms. That's the trouble today – no discipline.
Palmer (*sighing*) Yes, Higgins.
Higgins What are you reading?
Palmer *War and Peace*.
Higgins That's a big book. Tolstoy, isn't it?
Palmer Yes.
Higgins Yes, always wrote big books, Tolstoy. And that one was his life's work. Bit of a challenge (*He studies Palmer*) Do you expect to finish it?

Palmer Yes, why shouldn't I?

Higgins I must say it shows a confidence in the future. Knowing the reputation of this hospital I'd have chosen something shorter. (*He pauses*) Funny — I've known quite a few people who've started *War and Peace* but I've never known anyone who's actually finished it. I wonder why that is?

Palmer (*sharply*) Because people like you keep interrupting them.

Higgins Sorry, Charlie. I won't say another word. (*He turns his attention to Gary*) What are you doing, Gary?

Gary (*briefly*) I'm writing.

Higgins I can see that. (*He pauses*) What are you writing?

Gary I'm not telling you.

Higgins All right, if that's how you feel. As long as it's not poetry.

Palmer What's wrong with poetry? It's the expression of man's finest feelings.

Higgins Not now it isn't. (*He pauses*) I bet it's poetry and I bet it doesn't even rhyme.

Gary It doesn't have to rhyme. Dylan Thomas's poetry didn't rhyme.

Higgins That's because he was on a bottle of Scotch a day — his senses were clouded.

Palmer He wrote some fine poetry.

Higgins It would have been better if it had rhymed. What's yours about?

Gary I'm not writing poetry.

Higgins Is it about Christine?

Gary Why should it be about Christine?

Higgins I've seen the way you've been looking at her.

Gary Higgins, for the last time I'm not writing poetry. As a matter of fact, I'm keeping a diary.

Higgins (*staring*) A diary. You mean dates, appointments, meetings — that sort of thing?

Gary Well, it's a little more than that.

Higgins It would have to be. I mean, you're not going anywhere, are you? You're not doing anything. A cabbage would have more to write about.

Gary It's not like that. It's my thoughts and observations.

Palmer You mean your reflections on your life here and the interesting characters you've met.

Gary Well, sort of ...

Higgins You mean you're writing about us and the things we say?

Gary If it's of any interest.

Palmer Well, that lets you out, Higgins — you've never said anything interesting.

Higgins (*moving to Gary*) Let's have a look.

Gary No, it's a diary. It's private.

Higgins So is our conversation. Why can't I have a look?

Gary shuts the book away in his locker

Gary Now I wish I hadn't told you. Why can't you read your book?

Higgins Because it's dead boring. (*He returns to the table and picks up the book*) I found it in the day room. *Tangled Web* by Ethel P Dodds. A hospital romance. It's about this nurse. She becomes involved with Gerald, a patient. He's a slender young man with beautiful hands, white teeth and the darkest hair she's ever seen. She's worried about him but she tries to hide it. She keeps going outside and pressing her face against the wall.

Gary Why does she press her face against the wall?

Higgins She's fighting back the tears because she's a nurse. She's always doing that, or biting her lower lip, or digging her nails into the palms of her hands, and all the time her heart lurches and leaps beneath the starched apron.

Palmer And she's worried about Gerald. If I were Gerald I'd be worried about her. She sounds in a state of collapse.

Higgins She is. She's been tossed aside by rich playboy Brad Stevens, tanned, broad shouldered and better looking than any man deserves to be. He's just been admitted to Casualty after falling from his polo pony. But when she sees him he's not the same old Brad. The clean cut face looks worn and there are smudges of weariness under the eyes.

Palmer (*sighing*) I know how he feels.

Gary What did she do when she saw him?

Higgins The colour drained from her lips and she had to go out for some fresh air.

Palmer God. She's off again. She'll be pressing her face against the wall again in a minute. No wonder he tossed her aside.

Gary How does it finish?

Higgins I don't know yet.

Palmer I can tell you. Brad Stevens will get her. The young patient will probably die. (*He falls silent as he realizes what he has said*)

Palmer and Higgins exchange glances

Gary (*sharply*) Why should he?

Palmer What?

Gary Why should the young patient die?

Higgins and Palmer exchange another glance

Palmer (*uneasily*) Well, that's what happens in fiction — it's not real life.

Higgins It's only a story, Gary.

Gary joins them at the table and regards them suspiciously

(*Hastily*) Besides, I'm not so sure Brad Stevens will get her. Young Gerald's just told her that her eyes are the exact shade of emerald. That's made her think. And then there's Doctor Bentley-Carew. He's helping her to pick up the pieces.

Palmer Don't tell me she drops things as well.

Higgins He keeps kissing her on the forehead and knocking her hat askew. But she can't forget Brad Stevens and his mind-numbing kisses. She has to keep reminding herself that she's a nurse and not some cheap and ready thing.

Palmer Well, that's certainly fiction. She's not like any nurse I've met. I had a deep relationship with one once.

Higgins That must have been handy. You could discuss your symptoms and have a bit of "How's-your-father" at the same time.

Gary What sort of relationship?

Palmer Oh, it was wonderful. I'll never forget those nights. Intoxicating perfume, eyes like fire, skin the texture of silk ——

Higgins Well, that's enough about you: what was she like?

Palmer There was nothing starched about her, Higgins. The pictures fell from the wall on those nights.

Gary What do you mean, the pictures fell from the wall?

Palmer I wonder if Christine's like that.

Higgins Christine?

Palmer She's on tonight. I thought I might expose her to my particular brand of magnetic charm.

Gary What do you mean – the pictures fell from the wall?

Higgins Are you sure about this, Charlie? I mean you're not well.

Palmer I've told you – it doesn't seem to have affected that side of my nature.

Higgins Well, all I'm saying is ——

Gary What does he mean the pictures fell from the wall?

Higgins Do you mind, Gary? We're talking. All I'm saying is, Charlie — in your state of health you have to be careful. They say the energy required is equivalent to a four mile walk.

Palmer (*grinning*) Yes but it's more fun, Ray – and you don't wear your shoes out.

Gary (*staring*) What's equivalent to a four mile walk?

Palmer (*archly*) Can't you guess?

Gary (*frowning*) Why don't you leave her alone?

Palmer What was that?

Gary She has enough to cope with without that.

Palmer Without what?

Gary Without being mauled.

Palmer Mauled! I've never mauled anyone in my life. I'm not a mauler. You want to watch what you're saying.

Higgins (*sighing*) I wish you two would shut up. You're getting more neurotic everyday.

Palmer I'm not neurotic.

Gary Neither am I.

Higgins You mean you don't think you are. Did you know that one in three of the population suffers from some form of mental disorder? (*He looks at them*). It would appear we're above the national average …

Palmer What do you know about it?

Higgins I've made a study of psychiatry and I must say it's given me a greater understanding.

Palmer Of what?

Higgins Well, of you for a start.

Palmer There's nothing wrong with my mind.

Higgins Are you sure? Do you know the signs of mental instability? Touchy, restless, changeable, unpredictable, excitable, active, impulsive … (*He stares at Palmer*) Who does that remind you of?

Gary He's not active.

Higgins No but six out of seven's not bad. I'd love to analyse him.

Palmer Well, you're not going to.

Gary You can analyse me if you like, Ray. I'm not afraid.

Higgins Then we'll start with a little word association. It can be very revealing. I say a word and you say anything that comes into your head. Right?

Gary Left.

Higgins I haven't started yet. Here we go.

Higgins commences a list of words putting some stress on their sexual implications

Higgins Leg.

Gary Table.

Higgins Body.

Gary Belt.

Higgins Breast.

Gary Plate.

Higgins (*frowning*) Sex.

Gary Male.

Palmer Oh yes ….

Higgins (*desperately*) Girl.

Gary Guide.

Higgins Love.

Gary Fifteen.

Higgins Pardon?

Gary Granted.

Higgins No, what do you mean — fifteen?

Gary Love – fifteen.

Higgins Oh. (*Slowly*) Kiss.

Gary Goodbye.

Higgins Date.

Gary Fig.

Higgins Brassière.

Gary Night watchman.

Higgins (*with great emphasis*) Affair.

Gary Dodgems.

Higgins Dodgems! (*Defeated*) Blimey! Well, that's the worst case of sexual repression I've ever come across.

Palmer You didn't need a test to find that out.

Gary At least I wasn't afraid to take it.

Palmer (*slyly*) All right, Higgins. Test me.

Higgins Here we go then. Blue.

Palmer (*archly*) Gardenia.

Higgins Black.

Palmer Chiffon.

Higgins Red.

Palmer Lips.

Higgins White.

Palmer Sheets.

Higgins Brown.

Palmer Flesh.

Higgins (*impressed*) Oh dear. Oh dear. Woman.

Palmer Nurse.

Higgins Bed.

Palmer Love.

Higgins Sex.

Palmer Christine.

Gary What!

Palmer Well, what's the diagnosis, Higgins?

Higgins Well, off the cuff I'd say you are sexually obsessed with the nursing profession probably due to your years at boarding school where the only female influence was Matron. This now manifests itself in repeated visits to hospital and this current infatuation with Christine.

Gary Well, he'd better forget it.

Palmer Why should I?

Gary Because if you don't — I'll report you and they'll put you in a side ward where you belong.

Gary slams out

Palmer What's got into him?

Higgins I think he's planning a four mile walk in that direction himself.

Palmer No. He's a prig. You've seen his face when sex is mentioned. It's as if someone's dangled a dead kipper under his nose.

Higgins You're forgetting something. (*He lowers his voice*) The poor bugger's on the way out. Perhaps he wants to do it before it's too late.

Palmer He seems to be moving around reasonably well.

Higgins He's probably in remission.

Palmer You can't be sure. How do we know?

Higgins The orderly said he was in this ward.

Palmer I'm in this ward.

Higgins And in the end bed.

Palmer I'm in an end bed.

Higgins And he's young.

Palmer Well, I'm young. I'm only thirty-nine, Ray.

Higgins (*studying him*) You must have suffered a great deal.

Palmer What do you mean?

Higgins Charlie, you wouldn't pass for thirty-nine with a bag over your head. Besides, they don't call you by your first name – they always do that when you're handing in your pail. And you don't get any visitors. He had six round his bed this afternoon, two of them from Australia. And they were very demonstrative; that's a bad sign.

Palmer Higgins, I don't get any visitors because I've told them not to come. I don't want my friends to see me suffer.

Higgins Why not? They might enjoy it.

Palmer That's right. Have a go at me. You've been doing that ever since he arrived.

Higgins What do you mean?

Palmer Don't think I haven't noticed. Whispering together … ganging up on me.

Higgins Ganging up? I hardly know him.

Palmer You certainly don't. He's sly.

Higgins No, he isn't. What's got into you? I just feel sorry for him, that's all.

Palmer Perhaps you should feel sorry for yourself.

Higgins Why?

Palmer I thought Edie never came to see you. She was all over you yesterday, kissing and cuddling. I thought she was going to get into bed with you. Now that's what I call demonstrative. Perhaps she knows something. After all, you said Edie couldn't stand illness.

Higgins She can't. That wasn't Edie.

Palmer What?

Higgins That was Peg.

Palmer Peg?

Higgins Yeah, we met one night in Gateshead. She wanted to have a look round my lorry. I showed her inside the cab and one thing led to another. You know how it is.

Palmer Oh, I see. (*He pauses*) Well, suppose it is Gary. Do you think he knows?

Higgins He's been very quiet lately.

Palmer Perhaps they've told him.

Higgins One way to find out.

Palmer How?

Higgins Look in his diary.

Palmer You can't do that. It's an invasion of privacy.

Higgins So is recording our private conversations. Where did he put it? (*He opens Gary's drawer*) Here it is. (*He brings out the diary, opens it and reads*)

Palmer Higgins, you can't ... (*He stops. Curiously*) What does it say?

Higgins (*grinning*) Here's the last entry. (*He reads*) "P has been preening himself again this evening."

Palmer (*staring*) P? Who's P?

Higgins I'll give you one guess — Palmer. (*He reads*) "He's been combing the crumbs out of his moustache and studying his hair loss."

Palmer What!

Higgins (*reading*) "I suppose that means he'll be subjecting C to his nauseating approaches again tonight."

Palmer Nauseating!

Higgins (*reading*) "H says P is fatally ill but I'm not so sure — he seems to be getting stronger."

Palmer He sounds disappointed.

Higgins (*reading*) "But I can't help feeling sorry for him – he's a sad figure. Despite his incessant boasting he seems so alone."

Palmer Alone! Sorry for me!

Higgins (*reading*) "But in another way I envy him. At least he's done it. I listen to his tales of conquest and wonder what I've done with my life. P says he only regrets the opportunities he missed. How many opportunities have I missed? All of them. C came to me tonight and squeezed my hand. I'm sure she prefers me to P but I don't suppose I'll do anything about it ..." It sort of trails off there ...

Palmer (*angrily*) Prefers him. Of all the arrogance. Sad — I'm not sad.

Higgins No, he's the one who's sad, Charlie. You'll have to stand aside. Take your sleeping pill and forget about it.

Palmer Stand aside. Why?

Higgins He hasn't done it. You've done it.

Palmer Yes, and I'm going to do it again. Preening! My God!

Higgins He's jealous of your experience, Charlie. You've done everything; he's just a blank page waiting to be written on by life.

Palmer Well, he can remain a blank as far as I'm concerned. I could have any nurse in this hospital.

Higgins Yes, I know you could. Well, except Ranji I suppose.

Palmer (*grimly*) Squeezed his hand, did she? Well, we'll see what happens tonight.

Higgins You can't be serious.

Palmer I've never been more serious in my life.

Higgins But you're not up to it.

Palmer Aren't I? See and be amazed, Higgins.

Ranji enters

Ah, Ranji. You can tell Mr Gibbs I'm feeling much stronger. (*He glances at Higgins*) In fact I'm thinking of taking a little light exercise.

Ranji You should try yoga.

Palmer Yoga. I said I was feeling better. I didn't say I wanted tying in bloody knots.

Gibbs enters

Gibbs What's the matter with Palmer?

Ranji He said he wanted a little light exercise. I suggested yoga. It would help him to relax.

Gibbs Yoga.

Ranji He is very nervous and tense.

Gibbs Nervous and tense. Ranji, have you asked yourself why all my patients appear to be nervous and tense? Not very flattering, is it?

Ranji No, Mr Gibbs.

Gibbs Still, I think we can dispense with the wisdom of the East. Give him a Mogadon. Now let's have a look at you, Palmer … (*He looks into Palmer's eyes*)

Higgins looks over Gibbs's shoulder

(*Becoming aware of Higgins*) Higgins, I hope you don't think I'm pulling rank but do you mind if I examine Palmer first this evening?

Higgins Not at all. I think he's got anaemia.

Gibbs grunts

And his eyes are inflamed.

Gibbs I'll be inflamed if you don't get back into bed, Higgins. (*He consults Palmer's notes*) It does appear you're somewhat anaemic, Palmer.

Higgins What did I tell you?

Gibbs But this could be treated by your GP. I see you've refused a blood transfusion. Not a Jehovah's Witness, are you?

Palmer No, it's simply that I've managed to hang on to this particular brew and I wouldn't like to see it diluted.

Gibbs It wouldn't be diluted. It's only blood, Palmer.

Palmer Mr Gibbs, I am descended from the men who fought side by side with William at Hastings, who fought their way with bloodstained swords across the breadth of England. Who bowed to no man except their royal liege, whose cry was "God and the King". Who raised Henry Tudor to the throne and exiled the Stuarts. And you say it's only blood.

Gibbs (*stepping back nervously, then turning to Ranji*) Have we changed his medication?

Ranji Yes, Mr Gibbs.

Gibbs I think we need something stronger. (*He returns to Palmer*) How do you feel?

Palmer A little unusual.

Gibbs But then you're an unusual person, Palmer.

Palmer That's true. And this enforced idleness doesn't suit an active man. (*He glances at Higgins*) That's why I wondered if I could take a little exercise.

Gibbs I don't see why not.

Palmer Perhaps even a four mile walk?

Gibbs That's a little ambitious. I think you'd find that rather tiring.

Palmer (*with another glance at Higgins*) On the contrary I think it might prove quite invigorating.

Higgins (*shaking his head*) On the other hand he could be signing his death warrant.

Palmer Death warrant!

Gibbs Why do you think that, Higgins?

Higgins I just wonder if you've missed something.

Gibbs And what do you think I've missed?

Higgins (*after a dramatic pause*) Addison's disease.

Gibbs Addison's disease!

Higgins He has the classic symptoms: general lethargy, feeble heartbeat, patchy skin.

Palmer (*concerned*) Patchy skin.

Higgins All the signs of a deficiency in the adrenal cortex.

Gibbs Higgins, Addison's disease effects four people in a million.

Higgins He said he felt unusual; you can't get more unusual than that.

Gibbs Ranji, have you noticed any link, any common thread in Higgins' diagnosis?

Ranji No, Mr Gibbs.

Gibbs Use your powers of observation. Anaemia, adrenal cortex, Addison's disease. They all begin with A. (*He picks a book up from Higgins' locker*) Higgins has acquired a medical dictionary and is working through the letter A. Tomorrow it'll probably be Bronchitis – Botulism and Baghdad Button. Now, for God's sake leave the diagnosing to me, Higgins. (*He slams the book down*)

Gibbs exits followed by Ranji

Higgins Well, if he feels like that he can do his own diagnosing. I won't say another word. (*He pauses*) Did you notice his thyroid?

Palmer Shut up, Higgins. (*He takes out a comb and begins preening*)

Higgins watches him

(*Aware of Higgins' scrutiny*) I shall be drawing my curtains tonight — so no peeping. (*Witheringly*) Addison's disease.

Higgins Well, there's something wrong with you; you're almost yellow and your skin's hanging in folds.

Palmer Is it? (*He studies himself in the mirror*)

Higgins Yeah. I don't know what you've got arranged for tonight but I wouldn't make plans with a skin like that. (*He continues to study Palmer*) You haven't been abroad, have you?

Palmer Why?

Higgins Only it looks strangely like malaria.

Palmer Malaria!

Higgins Where did you go for your holidays?

Palmer Bournemouth.

Higgins There you are then.

Palmer What do you mean, there you are then? Higgins, to get malaria you have to be bitten by a mosquito.

Higgins That's right.

Palmer You don't get those sort of mosquitoes in Bournemouth.

Higgins That's what you think. What's down the road from Bournemouth? Southampton, the docks. When they open those holds you don't know what's going to come out. Suppose there's one reposing in a crate of bananas? Gets disturbed. It's a mild summer evening; it comes wafting down the coast road on a warm thermal current drawn to the bright lights of Bournemouth. Sees you on the terrace outside the Pavilion sipping a light ale. Goes into a dive. Bingo: from Uganda with love, straight in the back of the neck.

Palmer I think I'd have remembered that, Higgins. Besides, it rained all the time. Malaria. That's almost as ridiculous as Addison's disease. (*He pauses*) Hanging in folds?

Higgins You must have noticed the deterioration.

Palmer I thought it was just me. You can see it too.

Higgins You can't miss it. It's got worse since you came in. I know it's ridiculous but you look like someone who's spent too long in the tropics. That's what made me think of malaria.

Palmer I haven't been in the tropics.

Higgins I said it was ridiculous … (*He pauses*) Wait a minute. Before Christine came on here where was she working?

Palmer The isolation ward.

Higgins Isolation ward.

Palmer What's the matter?

Higgins That's infectious diseases, isn't it, Charlie?

Palmer Well, yes, but that was weeks ago.

Higgins Weeks ago. When we talk about infectious diseases we don't talk in weeks we talk in years. They're still finding bacteria from the Black Death.

Palmer (*appalled*) The Black Death!

Higgins Don't worry, you haven't got that; you get boils under your armpits. Wait a minute. Didn't Christine say they had a very serious case on the Isolation ward? He was turning yellow — skin in folds. Brought him in from Heathrow. Had to pass his food to him with tongs. Highly infectious.

Palmer Highly infectious?

Higgins And when he died, he had a coffin with windows in it …

Palmer Windows?

Higgins So that his family could look inside without lifting the lid — sort of like a business envelope. They said it was parrot fever …

Palmer Parrot fever. What are the symptoms?

Higgins You start repeating what people say.

Palmer What? You're doing it again, Higgins.

Higgins No, I was only joking. It's a virus passed on by the parrot which can lead to pneumonia — and death.

Palmer I haven't got that.

Higgins Of course not … well, perhaps a mild form.

Palmer Mild form. You're trying to frighten me.

Higgins (*shrugging*) It's your life. All I'm saying is why take the risk in your state of health. What you need is rest. And if she is a carrier …

Palmer A carrier … (*He hesitates*) Perhaps I should take my sleeping tablet …

Higgins Have mine as well. (*He hands Palmer his tablet*)

Palmer She'll be disappointed.

Higgins Of course she will. (*He moves to Gary's bed and picks up Gary's tablet*) She's attracted to you, I can see that. (*He returns to Palmer with Gary's tablet*) Have another one for luck.

Palmer What?

Higgins We don't want her disturbing you in the middle of the night, do we? Forcing herself on you — breathing all over you …

Palmer Breathing all … (*He reaches for the water jug*)

Christine enters

Christine How are you, Charlie?

Higgins He's just taking his tablets.

Christine Let me pour you some water. (*She pours some water into Palmer's glass*)

Palmer watches Christine apprehensively. She hands him the glass and Palmer stares at the contents almost as if he expects to see germs floating in the water. Christine moves to raise Palmer's pillows; he flinches and stares back at the water

Christine What's the matter?

Palmer It's stale — it's been standing. I'll … er … get some fresh …

Palmer exits hurriedly

Christine What's the matter with Charlie?

Higgins No idea. He's been edgy all day.

Christine Have you been winding him up?

Higgins As if I would. (*He returns to his book*)

Christine picks up the flowers and heads for the exit

Gary enters

Gary and Christine meet

Gary Christine.

Christine Hallo, Gary. I'm just doing the flowers. Would you like to help me?

Gary (*hesitating*) Er, no … I don't think I'm strong enough … I feel quite tired … I think I'll rest …

Christine Oh.

She exits

Gary moves to his bed. Higgins watches him. Gary catches Higgins's eye

Higgins You know, Gary you're going to miss a lot of fun in life if you act like that every time a woman speaks to you.
Gary I'm tired.
Higgins No, you're not. Now are you going to do something about it or not?

Christine enters and picks up more flowers

Gibbs enters. He stands regarding Christine silently

Christine (*turning and almost walking into Gibbs*) Mr Gibbs. You startled me. I didn't realize you were still here.
Gibbs The penalty for being a surgeon I'm afraid. Late hours … and loneliness.

Gibbs and Christine move downstage watched with interest by Higgins and Gary

Christine (*smiling*) Loneliness. You're not lonely.
Gibbs You'd be surprised, Christine. I find it very difficult to get close to people …
Christine You were pretty close to people at that party …
Gibbs (*archly*) Was I? (*He pauses*) I've been watching you Christine. I like the way you're shaping. Perhaps we could talk about your future …
Christine My future?
Gibbs You're wasted in here. You need … stretching … I —— (*He becomes aware of Higgins and Gary watching*) Perhaps we could talk about this in your office. (*He puts an affectionate arm on Christine's shoulder*)

Christine and Gibbs exit into the nurses' station

Higgins Did you see that? This is just like *Tangled Web*. And while you're fluttering your beautiful hands Gibbs is going to be knocking her hat askew and Palmer's going to be pursuing her with pantherish strides. Everywhere you look the colour's going to be draining from someone's lips or they'll be digging their nails into their palms.
Gary I never thought that stuff was true, Ray, hearts lurching and leaping, but it is.

Higgins There's nothing truer than cheap fiction, Gary.

There is the sound of a loud slap, off

Gibbs enters from the nurse's office looking furious and rubbing his cheek. He exits into the corridor

I think this could be your night, Gary.

Gary Suppose she prefers Palmer?

Higgins She doesn't. That's what's annoying him. He keeps asking "Mirror, mirror on the wall who is the fairest of us all?" And the answer keeps coming back the same, "Not you, my old cock". This is your chance. Get in there.

Gary Perhaps another night.

Higgins (*desperately*) There may not be another night.

Gary (*curiously*) What do you mean?

Higgins (*after a hesitation*) Well, look, Gary — none of us know what's going to happen when we come into these places. You have to face the possibility that you may not make it. And remember you've always regretted not doing more with your life.

Gary I really meant going abroad.

Higgins This beats going abroad.

Palmer enters as if in a dream. He is almost sleepwalking. He falls into bed and closes his eyes with a groan

Higgins gets out of bed. He switches off Palmer's light and pulls the blankets over him; then he returns to his own bed

Gary Ray, in *Tangled Web*, did the young patient die?

Higgins Young Gerald? No.

Gary What happened?

Higgins Well, Gerald had this friend, genial Jim Merryweather, an older man, kindly and thoughtful, who was suffering intense pain without a word of complaint. You know it's amazing how these characters resemble real people.

Gary What did Jim Merryweather do?

Higgins He eliminated his main rival. (*He glances across at the sleeping Palmer*) Brad Steven's eyes may be cloudy with desire but he won't be stirring tonight. He's been nobbled. So, in the words of Ethel P Dodds — ring that bell and enter the gates of ecstasy.

Gary You won't look.

Higgins Of course I won't look. Get on with it.

Gary (*after a hesitation*) What did Gerald do in the book?

Higgins Well, he rang the bell for the nurse and asked her to straighten his pillows. And then he said something in a very low voice, almost a whisper, so faint she had to place her adorable face against his lips. Then he gave her one.

Gary One what?

Higgins A kiss, full on the lips.

Gary What did she do?

Higgins She responded. Because he had something Brad Stevens couldn't give her.

Gary What was that?

Higgins His innocence.

Gary Suppose she tells me what to do with my innocence?

Higgins She won't.

Gary Suppose she slaps my face?

Higgins Gary, there aren't many advantages in being ill. You could probably count them on one hand. But one thing's certain. You don't get your face slapped. Now ring that bell. (*He switches off his light and settles down*)

Only Gary's bed is now illuminated

Gary rings the bell

  Christine enters. She straightens Palmer's bed and then moves to Gary

Christine (*bending over Gary*) You should be asleep. (*She straightens his pillows*)

Gary (*softly*) I can't sleep. Christine ... I ... (*His voice drops into a whisper*)

Christine What did you say, Gary? (*She bends low over him*)

Gary kisses Christine. She stares in surprise and then looks quickly around the ward. The ward is silent. She turns back to Gary. A longer kiss develops

There is a troubled groan from Palmer

Higgins' hand emerges from under the covers. He is giving a thumbs-up sign

CURTAIN

SCENE 2

The ward. Two days later. Lunchtime

Higgins and Gary are finishing a meal

Higgins (*sighing*) This is foul. Still, it's amazing what the stomach can digest — even tripe.

Gary (*doubtfully*) This isn't tripe — is it?

Higgins No but if it was tripe you'd be able to digest it which is amazing when you come to think about it.

Gary Why?

Higgins Because that's what tripe is: stomach lining. How is it we can digest tripe without digesting our stomachs? You'd think they'd both go the same way. In which case when we came to the pudding it would fall straight through.

Gary puts down his knife and fork

Of course you know what the answer is, don't you? Mucus.

Gary moves back to his bed

What's the matter?

Gary I'm not hungry.

Higgins (*putting his knife and fork down and sighing*) Neither am I. I've been off my food for days. Ever since I had that barium meal.

Gary What was it like?

Higgins Better than the steamed fish but only just. There's only one thing to be said in favour of a barium meal.

Gary What's that?

Higgins There's only one course.

Palmer enters. He is wearing blazer and flannels and looks well-groomed. He smiles self-consciously

Sorry, mate. No visitors. They're feeding the animals.

Gary It's Charlie!

Higgins So it is. I didn't recognize you with your clothes on, Charlie. (*He studies Palmer*) How do you feel?

Palmer Terrible.

Gary You don't look terrible.

Palmer You can't see beyond this blazer, can you, Gary?

Higgins Clothes maketh the man, Charlie.

Palmer Maketh me. They're probably all that's holding me up.

Gary Come on, Charlie, your blood pressure's normal, your pulse is normal, the palpitations have gone.

Palmer But not the red hot poker in the side, Gary — that's still there. They're discharging a sick man. And they're sending me back to an empty flat with nothing in the fridge.

Higgins (*considering*) I suppose there's always "Meals on Wheels".

Palmer (*shocked*) "Meals on Wheels!" I can't live on that. Besides, they'd never get it to me. I live ten floors up.

Higgins They could put it in the lift and you could press the button.

Palmer It would be cold before I got it. I can't survive on cold rice pudding. And suppose the lift breaks down? There are ten flights of stairs and I haven't got the strength back in my legs yet. They'll find a pile of bleached bones in my room next spring.

Gary You could have a red card to put in the window – to summon assistance.

Palmer I'm ten floors up. Who's going to see it; the bloody pigeons? It's not as if I can depend on my GP. He won't call. I have to shout my symptoms down the phone these days.

Higgins That's because you're a hypochondriac.

Palmer All right, Ray, I'm a hypochondriac but I'm a sick hypochondriac, that's the difference. It's all right for you. You'll be going home to a wife and family. I'm going back to an empty flat.

Gary (*mockingly*) I thought it would be full of your fashionable friends, Charlie, tucking into the wine and cheese.

Palmer To tell the truth, Gary, since I've been ill I've rather lost touch with my friends. That room's going to seem pretty empty after this.

Gary What about all those girlfriends?

Palmer Well, yes … the trouble is I'm sort of between girlfriends at the moment. I think I'd better have a word with Sister — sort out my medication.

Higgins Well, don't go without saying good-bye.

Palmer I won't.

He exits

Gary (*derisively*) Between girlfriends. I bet he's always between girl-friends.

Higgins Be fair, Gary. He does live ten floors up. It must be a bit of a challenge. By the time they've got there they're probably suffering from lack of oxygen.

Gary It's more likely to be boredom. Having to listen to all those symptoms. What a hypochondriac.

Higgins (*sharply*) It's not hypochondria, you heartless bugger — it's bloody loneliness.

Gary What's the matter?

Higgins Show a little charity. No one's perfect. You know, you've become quite unsympathetic since you had your end away.

Gary (*shocked*) Higgins! I haven't.

Higgins Haven't become unsympathetic or haven't had your end away?

Gary Both.

Higgins Oh, yes, you have. I don't know how you've managed it but you have. I can always tell. Hospital's certainly changed your life, hasn't it?

Palmer returns

Palmer Gary — Mr Gibbs wants to see you.

Gary Perhaps he's going to let me go home.

Gary exits

Higgins Poor little bugger. I wonder if they're going to give him the bad news.

Palmer I don't think so. Gibbs seemed far too cheerful.

Higgins That's because you're going.

Palmer Well, I just hope he doesn't have cause to regret it. I can hardly lift this suitcase.

Higgins You should have had that transfusion, Charlie.

Palmer (*sitting*) I have a confession to make, Ray. I had one last year – when my blood count was low.

Higgins You didn't say.

Palmer It's always worried me. I've never felt right since. I couldn't face another.

Higgins You think you may have picked something up? You don't have to worry. It's screened. I should know, I was a donor.

Palmer (*staring*) You?

Higgins Yeh.

Palmer You mean there are people going around with your blood inside them?

Higgins I suppose so.

Palmer Good heavens. You see, that's what worries me. Who was it? Who's in here with me?

Higgins I shouldn't worry about it. It could be anyone.

Palmer Not anyone, Ray. (*Proudly*) I'm an AB negative.

Higgins AB negative. That's very rare.

Palmer I'll say it's rare – three per cent of the population.

Higgins I know. I'm one of them.

Palmer You're an AB negative?

Higgins Yes, you don't have to be middle class, Charlie. And being an AB negative made me very useful as a donor.

Palmer (*after a pause*) Yes — (*He begins to look concerned*) Did — did you give blood here last year, Ray?

Higgins Yes. Why?

Palmer (*appalled*) It could have been you. I knew it didn't feel right.

Higgins You mean my blood's not good enough for you? That comes from good yeoman stock, mate. That blood was shed at Agincourt, and the Somme, and Anzio. And you throw it back in my face. Well, don't ask for any more; apart from the fact that I can't spare it, I don't care if you shrivel up like a prune.

Palmer I'm sorry, Ray, I didn't mean it like that. But we're not compatible, and I just don't feel right.

Higgins That's not why you don't feel right.

Palmer Then what is it?

Higgins Can you take it?

Palmer Yes.

Higgins looks cautiously about him and holds up his medical dictionary

Higgins (*in a low voice*) Hashimoto's disease.

Palmer Hashimoto's disease? They didn't say anything.

Higgins They haven't spotted it. It's quite rare.

Palmer Rare. Is it dangerous?

Higgins No. It's a deficiency in the thyroid gland. Just needs watching that's all.

Palmer But it is rare?

Higgins Yes.

Palmer (*pleased*) Hashimoto's disease. I knew there was something.

Higgins Just see your GP. He'll give you some tablets.

Palmer (*eagerly*) There are tablets?

Higgins Probably have to take them for the rest of your life.

Palmer (*delighted*) The rest of my life. (*Dreamily*) Hashimoto's disease.

Higgins (*mischievously*) There may be a society …

Palmer A society.

Higgins And travel concessions. Just say Hashimoto's disease and you go to the front of the queue. And if you're flying, you'll probably get Club Class …

Palmer Club Class. I wonder if this qualifies me for an ambulance?

Higgins Er, I wouldn't say anything to them around here. They'll be furious they haven't spotted it, and you know how jealous they can be.

Palmer Right. Hashimoto's disease. I'll see my GP about it. I knew it was something rare. Mind you, I don't know how I'm going to make it to the bus stop.

Higgins I thought you'd have a car, or are you between cars at the moment?

Palmer It's being serviced.

Higgins You'll need it.

Palmer Of course I'll need it. I have to look for a job.

Higgins Yes, I was forgetting – you're between jobs as well. Well, don't rush; get yourself fit first.

Palmer No, I won't rush. I'll probably get myself a villa on the Algarve for the summer or possibly a Mediterranean cruise.

Higgins (*studying Palmer*) Got enough for a taxi?

Palmer (*after a hesitation*) Well, actually, I am rather short at the moment …

Higgins   stuffs money into Palmer's top pocket

What's this?

Higgins What does it look like? It's money. I know you haven't seen it for some time but that's what they use out there.

Palmer There must be fifty pounds here, Ray.

Higgins Take it and shut up.

Palmer I'll pay you back.

Higgins Of course.

Palmer And I didn't mean that about your blood. It would have been a privilege.

Higgins Did you feel that before I bunged you the money or after?

Palmer I mean it, Ray.

Higgins Well, what are you waiting for? You know I hate long goodbyes.

Palmer (*lowering his voice*) I thought I'd say goodbye to Gary. According to you he may not be around much longer. Although I must say he doesn't look too bad to me.

Higgins I always said it was good for you.

Palmer What?

Higgins Sex.

Palmer What do you mean?

Higgins He did it, Charlie.

Palmer Did what?

Higgins Had his four mile walk.

Palmer (*shocked*) With Christine.

Higgins That's right.

Palmer I don't believe it. How did he manage it?

Higgins I don't know but we can soon find out.

Palmer How?

Higgins His diary. (*He takes the diary from Gary's cabinet*) It should be the last entry …

Palmer He wouldn't put that in his diary even if he knew how to spell it.

Higgins Not in as many words. But there could be a star or a cross or just "Yippee". Let's see. April 29. Here it is. "It happened." Simple words to describe an earth shattering event, Charlie. (*He reads*) "It was C's night off. I slipped out as arranged. We went to her room in the nurses' quarters. I now know what P meant when he said the pictures fell from the wall." (*He smiles*) Well, I think we can be very satisfied with that outcome, Charlie.

During the following, Higgins glances through the diary, not listening to Palmer. As the speech progresses, he reads more intently, his face grim

Palmer (*bitterly*) Well, I'm not. That could have been me, Ray, instead of which I slept for sixteen hours and I still can't feel my teeth. Why did I let you talk me into taking those pills? And don't say his need's greater than mine — the pictures haven't fallen from the walls in a long time …. (*He realizes that Higgins isn't listening*) What's the matter, Ray? (*He takes the diary from Higgins. Reading*) "April 20. I must be careful about keeping this diary. H has been watching me again. His insatiable curiosity is one of his worst features — next to his garrulousness. No doubt he has strong views about keeping a diary —he has about everything else. I think he talks so much to hide his fears. I think he's more afraid than the rest of us but it's a weak character that puts his fears on to others. He had a woman come to see him today — not his wife — rather tarty. He really should get his life sorted out before it's too late … " (*He looks up as if to smile*)

Higgins' face is thunderous

(*Seeing Higgins' look*) He didn't mean it.

Higgins Of course he meant it.

Palmer April 20, Ray. He hardly knew you. I didn't like you at first. You grow on people.

Higgins Just put it back, will you?

Palmer returns the diary to Gary's cabinet

Ranji enters

Ranji Come along, my dear Palmer. You're going home.

Palmer Perhaps if I had an ambulance?

Ranji You don't need an ambulance. You only live down the road.

Palmer Well, possibly a wheelchair.

Ranji You don't need one.

Palmer (*after a pause*) What about a walking stick?

Ranji It's not necessary.

Palmer Well, perhaps you could carry my case as far as the lift.

Ranji No. You're going out of here on your own two feet — without any assistance. It'll be good for your confidence.

Gary enters. He looks stunned. He sits on his bed

The others watch him. There's a pregnant silence

Gary I've had some news.

Palmer What is it?

Gary I'm all right.

Higgins What?

Gary I've made a complete recovery. I can't believe it.

Higgins (*quietly*) Neither can I. (*He turns his back on Gary*)

Gary Gibbs said the complications were nothing serious after all. He reckons I'll be back at work in a week. Christine's going to give me a lift home. I can't wait to see my mother's face.

Palmer (*smiling*) I'm sure it'll be a picture, Gary. (*He moves to Higgins*) I'll be in to see you, Ray.

Higgins I wouldn't bother — I'll be out myself soon.

Palmer But the money ...

Higgins Forget it.

Palmer No, I can't forget it, Ray. I always pay my debts.

Gary (*looking across curiously*) What's all that about?

Higgins (*turns sharply*) What's the matter? Curious? You should watch that; it could be a vice if not controlled. (*He turns back to Palmer*) No, I shall probably be out tomorrow, right, Ranji?

Ranji Well, not tomorrow, Ray. Mr Gibbs wants to discuss a new course of treatment.

Higgins (*sighing*) A new course of treatment.

Ranji And now you have to see Mr McIver. I'll get a chair.

Ranji exits

Palmer (*smiling*) He called you Ray.

Higgins What?

Palmer Ranji called you Ray. He's never done that before. And you're getting a chair.

Higgins Well, as you say, I grow on people.

Palmer Look after yourself.
Higgins I don't have to – I'm in hospital.

Ranji enters with the wheelchair

Gary (*moving towards Higgins*) I'll probably be gone by the time you get
back, Ray … (*He holds out his hand*)

*Higgins gets into the chair without a word. Gary retracts his hand and then
holds it out again. Higgins ignores it and becomes busy with the wheelchair*

I know you hate goodbyes but ——
Higgins Not on this occasion I don't.
Gary (*staring*) What?
Higgins Goodbye.
Gary Is that all you've got to say?
Higgins Yes. I mean I don't have to talk all the time. I do enjoy conversation
— I feel it puts us above the animals — but it's not essential to my well-
being. I can enjoy moments of repose and I shall enjoy them when you've
gone. To tell the truth I've always found you rather intrusive.
Gary Intrusive.
Higgins Yes, and from now on I shall sit and regard life in silent contemplation
— and you can put that in your bleeding diary. Ranji.

Ranji pushes Higgins through the door and off

Gary stares after him in shocked surprise

CURTAIN

SCENE 3

The ward. Evening

The curtains are drawn around the bed L and a young man lies in it

Higgins is sitting alone at the table reading

*Gibbs enters studying some notes. He regards Higgins for a moment and
hesitates*

Higgins throws the book down with a sigh

Gibbs Good book?

Higgins Very few surprises there. Brad Stevens married his nurse — they were last seen passing under an arch of polo mallets. Dr Bentley-Carew, having been spurned, turned all his energies to curing the creeping paralysis that was threatening young Gerald's concert career. Gerald ended up playing at Carnegie Hall and Doctor Bentley-Carew won the Nobel Prize for Medicine.

Gibbs Happy ending all round then.

Higgins Not entirely. Genial Jim Merryweather went the way of all flesh in chapter thirteen. The last sight of Genial Jim was a pair of pale hands waving goodbye over the blankets … (*He stares at Gibbs curiously*) Did you want me for something?

Gibbs (*sitting*) No, I just wanted a few words, Ray.

Higgins Ray. This is unexpected, doctor. Is this the celebrated bedside manner we've heard so much about? You're not going to hold my hand, are you?

Gibbs (*smiling*) No.

Higgins Well, that's a relief.

Gibbs I've had a meeting with Mr McIver: he's completed his tests and …

Higgins Yes.

Gibbs I'm afraid the prognosis isn't good. The obstruction has become more advanced and there are secondary indications ...

Higgins (*considering*) This obstruction — it couldn't be a swab, could it?

Gibbs No, I'm afraid not. And in view of its advanced state we don't consider further surgery an option. I hope this isn't too much of a shock.

Higgins Not after you called me Ray. I knew I was in trouble.

Gibbs There's still hope, Ray, but there's a battle to be fought. We're planning an intensive course of chemotherapy ——

Higgins I'm going to lose my hair, aren't I?

Gibbs There are some side effects but in your case I think they're worth it. The resolve of the patient is an important factor in these cases.

Higgins My resolve is somewhere in my boots at the moment.

Gibbs That'll pass. Now if you prefer to go home and attend as a day patient ——

Higgins Go home? Do me a favour. With a wife who can't stand illness, four kids and a mother-in-law who worships the ground that's coming to me?

Gibbs Then it's better if you stay in here for the time being. (*He smiles*) We don't need the bed. And we've got quite used to having you around. (*He stands*) There are probably quite a few things you'll want to ask me. We'll talk again.

Higgins I'm not wearing a wig. You never know where you are with one of those. You're out to dinner one night — everyone saying how nice your hair looks — the waiter leans over you, and there it is, floating in the soup.

Gibbs It's not obligatory but what you must do is give up smoking.

Higgins Wait a minute. One thing at a time. I've already cut out the jogging. And you know I like a cigarette.

Gibbs (*awkwardly*) Yes, and I wondered if this might help to get you off the cigarettes. (*He produces a small case and hands it to Higgins*)

Higgins (*opening the case*) It's a pipe.

Gibbs Er, yes.

Higgins You bought this?

Gibbs Yes.

Higgins For me?

Gibbs I thought if you just stuck it in your mouth every time you felt like a smoke … it might help. That's how I gave up. Good-night, Ray.

Gibbs exits

Higgins stares after him in surprise. He sticks the pipe in his mouth

Higgins (*softly*) I'm H.A.P.P.Y.

Christine enters and disappears behind the curtains

Higgins watches intently

Christine emerges

Higgins How is he?

Christine He's comfortable.

Higgins Well, I don't like the look of him.

Christine It's some sort of paralysis.

Higgins It's Barrè's Syndrome.

Christine Is it?

Higgins It's a virus in the bloodstream; quite rare. We're lucky to come across it.

Christine I don't think he'd agree with you.

During the following, Christine strips Gary's bed

Higgins He'll need to have his blood changed.

Christine He's had a transfusion. He's come to us for minor surgery.

Higgins Well, at least they're working on the right lines. I was beginning to despair of this hospital.

Dance music plays, off

What's that?

Christine They're having a dance at the nurses' home. I'm going later. Is it disturbing you?

Higgins No, just as long as they don't play *The Last Tango*.

Christine picks up Gary's diary from his cabinet and begins reading it

Higgins What's that?

Christine It's Gary's diary. It was on his locker. He must have forgotten it.

Higgins (*uneasily*) You shouldn't be reading that — not another person's diary.

Christine (*looking up*) What does it mean? The pictures fell from the wall?

Higgins I've no idea and I'm not interested.

Christine I thought you liked Gary.

Higgins Did you? Well, you're wrong. There are some people you just don't warm to.

Christine He doesn't feel the same about you.

Higgins (*grimly*) Doesn't he?

Christine Listen to this last entry. (*She reads*) "I'm waiting for Christine to take me home. I can admit to myself now that I never thought I'd leave here. I thought I was going to die."

Higgins Look, I'm not interested.

Christine (*reading*) "I shall miss those two. Charlie with his superficial poise and his deep vulnerability and Ray with his grim sense of humour and his essential humanity —— "

Higgins (*staring*) Essential what?

Christine Humanity. (*She reads*) "He's just told me off for being superior about Charlie and he was right. Now he won't say goodbye. I must have upset him in some way. I'm sorry. I was wrong about him. If I ever become a writer —— "

Higgins A what?

Christine He wants to become a writer.

Higgins A writer! He couldn't leave a note for the milkman.

Christine (*reading*) " If I ever become a writer I'll write about men like Higgins. He'll always be in my work. He'll never die — not while I'm alive …" Isn't that nice?

Higgins It's a load of tripe. (*He pauses*) Let's have a look.

Christine smiles and hands Higgins the diary

She exits with the sheets

Higgins studies the diary

Palmer appears at the door. He is eating from a bag of grapes

Higgins (*putting the book down*) Bloody hell. What are you doing here?

Palmer I'm visiting you.

Higgins Thank God. I thought you'd collapsed again.

Palmer I've brought you some grapes. (*He eats another grape*)

Higgins Well, save me one, won't you. (*He takes a grape*)

Palmer (*sitting*) You look pale. How do you feel?

Higgins Bored. I feel like running stark naked through Geriatrics shouting "Who's for press-ups?"

Palmer (*nodding towards the curtains*) What's the matter with him?

Higgins Barrè's Syndrome. Touch and go …

Palmer (*significantly*) The end bed. You know we heard that rumour that someone was going to pop his clogs in here? I've found out who they were talking about.

Higgins (*stiffening*) Who was that?

Palmer Old Seymour.

Higgins (*relaxing*) Get away.

Palmer Died yesterday.

Higgins Poor bugger. (*He pauses*) Well, what's it like out there?

Palmer You wouldn't like it, Ray. It's all bustle. I was jostled several times on the way here.

Higgins There should be armbands for people just out of hospital.

Palmer I don't need an armband. I look terrible. A little old lady helped me across the road.

Higgins Still, you're out.

Palmer It wasn't much of a homecoming, Ray. The flat was a mess and I hadn't even got the strength for a little light dusting. And I found I'd left two kippers on the kitchen table the day I came in. The stench was terrible … (*He glances at Gary's diary*) What's that?

Higgins Gary's diary; he forgot it.

Palmer Any more about me?

Higgins (*smiling*) I wouldn't advise you to read it. You may have a superficial poise but you are deeply vulnerable.

Gary enters

Higgin's smile fades

Gary looks at Higgins uncertainly

Higgins (*coldly*) What do you want?

Gary I was just passing through and ...

Higgins Yeah?

Gary I wondered how you were.

Higgins Never felt better. Must be the peace and quiet.

Gary I mean what did Mr McIver say — about the tests?

Higgins Nothing to worry about. Just got to give up smoking, that's all.

Gary Do you think you can do it?

Higgins Of course I can. With my willpower it's a foregone conclusion.

Gary Yes, of course … (*He glances across at the curtains*) What's the matter with him?

Palmer Barrè's Syndrome. Touch and go.

Gary Well, I suppose I'd better … (*He begins to move off*)

Higgins Taking Christine to the dance?

Gary Yes. I'm dreading it.

Higgins Why

Gary I can't dance. I've no sense of rhythm.

Higgins That was never my problem. I was a tasty mover.

Gary Were you?

Higgins You should have seen me in those days. Hammersmith Palais, Strand Lyceum. With a gabardine drape suit, two inch crepe soles, and my D.A. I was the business.

Gary What's a D.A.?

Higgins (*shocked*) Duck's Arse. Don't you know anything? (*He sighs*) I was a sight to behold in those days. (*Sadly*) Not like now.

Gary (*sympathetically*) You were joined up properly then, Ray.

Higgins That's true.

Christine enters

Christine Ready, Gary?

Gary Yes. (*He hesitates*) Well, see you, Ray.

Higgins You're forgetting your diary.

Gary Oh, yes. Thanks. (*He takes the diary*)

Higgins Gary, if you're going to keep a diary let me give you a word of advice. Do what Sam Pepys did.

Gary What was that?

Higgins Write in shorthand, so that if it does happen to fall open and someone does inadvertently take a butcher's, no harm done.

Gary I didn't know he did that.

Higgins Oh yes. That's why Mrs Pepys never knew what was going on. It came as a total surprise when she found he was having it off with the housemaid.

Gary I'll remember that, Ray. I'll be in to see you … (*He holds out his hand*)

Higgins (*regarding Gary's hand for a moment and then taking it*) Why not? I'm not going anywhere.

Gary Right. See you later, Charlie.

Gary exits with Christine

Higgins (*grinning*) The crafty little devil. He didn't forget that diary.
Palmer You mean he wanted you to read it?
Higgins That was the idea.
Palmer Funny old world. Well, I'd better be going, Ray …
Higgins Wait a minute. What did he mean, see you later?
Palmer I'm going to the dance with them.
Higgins (*grinning*) So that's it. You're going to get yourself a nurse, aren't you?
Palmer I hadn't really thought about it.
Higgins Hadn't you? All those nurses. If you were to collapse in there think of the rush for the mouth to mouth resuscitation.

Palmer smiles and does a twirl on his way to the door

Palmer You know I've got the feeling this might be my lucky night, Ray.
Higgins (*with a sly smile*) Don't be too sure, Charlie. (*He sniffs*) You haven't quite lost the smell of those kippers ….
Palmer (*sniffing, then groaning*) Oh, no.

He exits

Ranji enters, slipping a coat on

Ranji Do you want anything, Ray?
Higgins No. Going off now?
Ranji Yes – it's been a long day. Twelve hours.
Higgins You're lucky you're not a patient. We have to do twenty-four – and no union.
Ranji (*smiling*) 'Night, Ray.
Higgins 'Night, mate.

Ranji exits

The dance music swells in volume

Higgins listens for a moment. He begins to dance around the room with an imaginary partner. He doubles up with pain. He takes a pillow from the bed and holds it to him. He continues to dance, at first painfully, then growing in confidence. Soon he is dancing in great style

Gibbs enters

They regard each other

Gibbs (*smiling*) Ray, do you think you can still those dancing feet? We don't want to disturb our patient.

Higgins How is he?

Gibbs It's Guillain Barrè's Syndrome.

Higgins That's what I thought.

Gibbs Well, I'm glad we agree on a diagnosis at last.

Higgins Anything I can do to help?

Gibbs Yes, there is something you can do. The virus attacks the central nervous system. The paralysis should recede but he needs stimulation – encouragement. (*With heavy irony*) I think he needs your particular brand of cheery optimism.

Higgins (*suspiciously*) Cheery optimism?

Gibbs (*smiling*) Good-night, Ray.

Gibbs exits

Higgins moves and opens the curtains around the bed

The young man is leaning back against the pillows staring into space

Higgins Hallo. Welcome to Jack the Ripper ward. No joke, is it? Still, there's one thing about being in hospital you can always find someone worse off than yourself. Me, for example. (*He pauses*) Do you want to see something horrible? I mean, do you want to see something really horrible ....? (*He opens his dressing-gown*) If God had meant this to happen he'd have given us zip fasteners ...

The young man groans

(*Turning away and grinning*) I think I'm getting through ...

CURTAIN

FURNITURE AND PROPERTY LIST

ACT I
SCENE 1

On stage: Three beds. *On* UR *bed:* bag of fruit, including orange, bottle in fancy
        wrapper, teddy bear
        Three cabinets. *On them:* flowers, jugs of water, glasses, get well cards,
        bedside lamps. *On cabinet by bed* L: mirror. *In cabinet by bed* L:
        mobile phone. *On cabinet by bed* C: medical dictionary. *In cabinet*
        by bed C: cigarettes, lighter
        Table
        Chairs

Check: Curtains drawn round bed L

Off stage: Bowl, shaving utensils (**Ranji**)
        Chart (**Christine**)
        Patient's consent form, pen (**Ranji**)
        Razor (**Christine**)
        Tablet (**Christine**)
        Small bag (**Gary**)
        Trolley (**Porter**)
        Surgical gown (**Christine**)

SCENE 2

Set: Pack of cards for **Palmer**
        On cabinet C: magazine, jug of clean water for **Higgins**

Strike: Bowl, shaving utensils, razor, small bag

Off stage: Small tape recorder (**Christine**)
        Blood test equipment on tray (**Ranji**)
        Kidney donor card (**Ranji**)

ACT II

SCENE 1

Re-set: Flowers

Set: *On each cabinet*: sleeping tablet
                Diary and pen for **Gary**
                Books for **Higgins** and **Palmer**

Personal: **Palmer**: comb

SCENE 2

Re-set: *On cabinet by bed* UR: **Gary**'s diary

Set: Plates, food, cutlery for **Higgins** and **Gary**

Off stage: Wheelchair (**Ranji**)

Personal: **Higgins**: money

SCENE 3

Re-set: *On cabinet by bed* UR: **Gary**'s diary

Set: Book for **Higgins**

Strike: Plates, food, cutlery

Off stage: Notes, pipe (**Gibbs**)
                Bag of grapes (**Palmer**)

www.ingramcontent.com/pod-product-compliance
Ingram Content Group UK Ltd.
Pitfield, Milton Keynes, MK11 3LW, UK
UKHW020935300925
3101IPUK00020B/73

9 780573 017957